Slow Cooker Favorites

CHICKEN

150+ EASY, DELICIOUS SLOW COOKER RECIPES,
from Hot Chicken Buffalo Bites and Chicken Parmesan to Teriyaki Chicken

Adams Media
New York   London   Toronto   Sydney   New Delhi

Aadamsmedia

Adams Media
An Imprint of Simon & Schuster, Inc.
57 Littlefield Street
Avon, Massachusetts 02322

First Adams Media trade paperback edition SEPTEMBER 2017

ADAMS MEDIA and colophon are trademarks of Simon and Schuster.

For information about special discounts for bulk purchases, please contact Simon & Schuster Special Sales at 1-866-506-1949 or business@simonandschuster.com.

The Simon & Schuster Speakers Bureau can bring authors to your live event. For more information or to book an event contact the Simon & Schuster Speakers Bureau at 1-866-248-3049 or visit our website at www.simonspeakers.com.

Interior design by Colleen Cunningham

Manufactured in the United States of America

10 9 8 7 6 5 4 3 2 1

Library of Congress Cataloging-in-Publication Data
Slow cooker favorites: chicken.
Avon, Massachusetts: Adams Media, 2017.
Series: Slow cooker favorites.
Includes index.
LCCN 2017020012 (print) | LCCN 2017021715
(ebook) | ISBN 9781507204696 (pb) |
ISBN 9781507204702 (ebook)
LCSH: Electric cooking, Slow. | Cooking (Chicken) |
LCGFT: Cookbooks.
LCC TX827 (ebook) | LCC TX827 .C47 2017 (print) |
DDC 641.6/65--dc23
LC record available at
https://lccn.loc.gov/2017020012

ISBN 978-1-5072-0469-6
ISBN 978-1-5072-0470-2 (ebook)

Always follow safety and comonsense cooking protocols while using kitchen utensils, operating ovens and stoves, and handling uncooked food. If children are assisting in the preparation of any recipe, they should always be supervised by an adult.

Contents

7   **INTRODUCTION**

9   **CHAPTER 1: SLOW COOKER BASICS**

17   **CHAPTER 2: EASY ESSENTIAL CHICKEN RECIPES**

18   Chicken Stock

19   Chicken Broth

20   "Precooked" Chicken

20   Poached Chicken

21   Rotisserie-Style Chicken

22   Roast Chicken

22   Foolproof Chicken

23   Chicken Braised in Beer

23   Steamed Chicken Sandwich

24   Spicy Plum Chicken

25   Mushroom Chicken Breast

26   Chicken in Onion-Mushroom Gravy

27   Spiced Apple Cider Chicken

27   Spicy Roasted Chicken Breast

28   Wild Rice–Stuffed Chicken Breast Cutlets

29   Chicken and Gherkin Sandwich

29   Ground Chicken and Carrot Quiche

31   **CHAPTER 3: APPETIZERS**

32   Stuffed Grape Leaves

33   Hot Chicken Buffalo Bites

33   Chicken Bites

34   Honey Mustard Chicken Fingers

35   Chicken Meatballs in a Hawaiian-Inspired Sauce

36   Light and Creamy Swedish Meatballs

37   Coconut Chicken Fingers

38   Curried Chicken Meatballs with Tomatoes

39   Curried Chicken Dip

40   Ground Chicken Tomato Sauce

41   Chicken Chowder

41   Chicken Tetrazzini

42   Spicy Buffalo Nuggets with Ranch Dressing

43   **CHAPTER 4: WINGS AND DRUMSTICKS**

44   Sticky Honey Wings

44   Green Curry Wings

45   Buffalo Chicken Wings

45   Sassy and Sweet Chicken Wings

46   Tandoori Chicken Wings

47   Green Chutney Wings

47   Pineapple Teriyaki Drumsticks

48   Gluten-Free "Shake It and Bake It" Drumsticks

49   Honey-Glazed Chicken Drumsticks

50   Chicken Drumsticks with Gluten-Free Stuffing

51 CHAPTER 5: SOUPS

52 Chicken Noodle Soup

53 Comforting Chicken and Rice Soup

54 Tortilla Soup

55 Chicken Vegetable Soup

55 Greek-Style Orzo and Spinach Soup

56 Murghi ka Shorba (Chicken Soup)

57 Greek Lemon-Chicken Soup

58 Aromatic Chicken Rice Soup

58 Simple Ground Chicken and Vegetable Soup

59 Tlalpeño Soup

59 Chicken Congee

60 Vietnamese Cucumber Soup

61 Chicken Mulligatawny Soup

62 Chicken Soup with Lukshen (Noodles)

63 Chicken and Wild Rice Soup

64 Herbed Chicken and Vegetable Soup

65 CHAPTER 6: CHILI AND STEWS

66 Fiery Chicken Chili

67 Lean Green Chili

68 Spicy Sausage Chili

68 California Chili

69 Summer Chili

70 Chicken Chili Verde

71 Chicken and Sweet Potato Stew

71 Chicken Corn Chowder

72 Eastern North Carolina Brunswick Stew

73 Creamy Chicken Stew

74 Chicken and Mushroom Stew

74 Tuscan Chicken and Sausage Stew

75 Rosemary-Thyme Stew

76 Easy Chicken and Rice Chili

77 Chicken-Tomatillo Chili

78 Chicken Stew with Meat Sauce

79 CHAPTER 7: COMFORTING FAVORITES

80 Chicken and Dumplings

81 No-Crust Chicken Potpie

81 Cinnamon Chicken Pasta

82 Biscuit-Topped Chicken Pie

83 Chicken and Gravy

83 Easy Chicken and Dressing

84 Scalloped Chicken

84 Chicken Stroganoff

85 Chicken Cacciatore

86 Chicken in Lemon Sauce

87 Chicken, Broccoli, and Rice Casserole

88 Chicken Paprikash

89 Creamy Chicken in a Mushroom and White Wine Sauce

90 Barbecue Chicken

90 Honey-Mustard Chicken

91 CHAPTER 8: CLASSIC AMERICAN DISHES

92 Creole Chicken and Vegetables

93 Hawaiian Chicken

94 Barbecue Chicken and Beans

95 Sweet and Spicy Pulled Chicken

95 Buffalo Chicken Sandwich Filling

96 Ground Chicken Joes

97 Chicken Tenders

97 Saucy Brown Sugar Chicken

98 Molasses Barbecue Chicken

99 Cajun Chicken and Shrimp Creole

100 Chicken Taco Filling

101 Enchilada Filling, Paleo Style

102 Salsa Chicken

102 Chili Beer Chicken

103 CHAPTER 9: ASIAN-INSPIRED DISHES

104 Teriyaki Chicken

104 Coconut Mango Spiced Chicken

105 Curried Chicken in Coconut Milk

105 Curried Coconut Chicken with Rice

106 Thai Curried Chicken

107 Thai-Influenced Braised Chicken Thighs

107 Thai Peanut Chicken

108 Ginger Caramelized Chicken

109 Orange Chicken

110 Chicken with Mango-Lime Sauce

110 Chicken in Plum Sauce

111 Almond Chicken

112 Asian-Spiced Chicken Breast

112 Almond Chicken Spinach Rolls

113 CHAPTER 10: INDIAN-INSPIRED DISHES

114 Chicken Makhani

115 Goan Chicken Curry

115 "Teekha" Peanut Chicken

116 Chicken Tikka Masala

117 Almond-Flavored Chicken (Badami Murgh)

118 Chicken Curry with Red Potatoes

119 Chicken in a Creamy Sauce (Murgh Korma)

120 Chili Coconut Chicken (Mangalorian Murgh Gassi)

121 Coriander Chicken (Dhaniye Wala Murgh)

122 Fenugreek-Flavored Chicken (Murgh Methiwala)

123 Ginger-Flavored Chicken Curry (Murgh Adraki)

124 Garlic Chicken (Lehsun Wala)

125 Chicken with Pickling Spices (Murgh Achari)

126 Murgh Musallam

127 Slow Cooker Tandoori Chicken

128 Spiced Chicken in Green Curry (Murgh Hariyali)

129 Indian Chicken with Chickpea Sauce

131 CHAPTER 11: ITALIAN-INSPIRED DISHES

132 Shortcut Chicken Parmesan

132 Pesto Chicken

133 Chicken Parmesan

133 Chicken Ragu

134 Tomato and Chicken Sausage Sauce

134 Chicken Saltimbocca

135 Cabbage Rollatini

136 Tuscan Chicken

136 Italian Chicken

137 Slow Cooker Chicken with Green Beans

137 Chicken Alfredo Pasta

138 Chicken Pesto Polenta

139 Tuscan Chicken and White Beans

140 Chicken Piccata

141 Chicken Meatball Sun-Dried Tomato Sauce

142 Italian Chicken Meatloaf

143 CHAPTER 12: MEDITERRANEAN-INSPIRED DISHES

144 Roast Chicken with Lemon and Artichokes

145 Chicken and Artichokes

145 Mediterranean Chicken Casserole

146 Spicy Olive Chicken

147 Sun-Dried Tomato and Feta–Stuffed Chicken

148 Balsamic Chicken and Spinach

148 Chicken Fricassee

149 Rosemary Chicken with Potatoes

150 Sage Ricotta Chicken Breasts

151 Lemony Roast Chicken

152 Chicken Cutlets with Red Onion Sauce

152 Five-Ingredient Greek Chicken

153 Slow-Roasted Chicken with Potatoes, Parsnips, and Onions

154 Chicken Budapest

155 CHAPTER 13: INTERNATIONAL FAVORITES

156 Caribbean Chicken Curry

157 Spanish Chicken and Rice

158 Peruvian Roast Chicken with Red Potatoes

159 Peruvian Chicken with Aji Verde

160 Chicken with Figs

161 Moroccan Chicken

162 Jerk Chicken

162 Ethiopian Chicken Stew

163 Tarragon Chicken

164 Filipino Chicken Adobo

164 Chicken in Onion Sauce

165 South African–Style Chicken

166 Tamales with Chicken and Olives

167 APPENDIX A: EQUIPMENT SOURCES

168 APPENDIX B: US/METRIC CONVERSION CHART

169 INDEX

Introduction

Are you sick of cleaning up a mountain of dirty dishes? Looking to serve a crowd? Does the simple act of eating a home-cooked meal seem like a luxury?

If this sounds familiar, it's time for you to plug in your slow cooker and make a hot meal a priority—not a chore.

With a slow cooker, you can create everything from appetizers to soups and stews to flavorful entrees and you don't have to worry about spending hours—or much time at all—in the kitchen. Just drop in your ingredients, turn on the slow cooker, and you're out the door with a delicious dinner guaranteed to greet you when you get home.

In *Slow Cooker Favorites: Chicken*, you'll find more than 150 chicken-based slow cooker recipes that make dinnertime easy, inexpensive, and incredibly versatile. This flavor-packed protein gives you dishes from a variety of cuisines—Mediterranean, Italian, Asian, and Indian—and even serves up a number of American favorites like Barbecue Chicken and Beans, Chicken Tenders, and Buffalo Chicken Sandwich Filling. You'll also find a chapter that gives you the rundown on how to use, clean, and store your slow cooker and information on how to customize your chicken recipes once you get the hang of using this appliance.

So whether you're craving Chicken Tikka Masala, Chicken Saltimbocca, Spanish Chicken and Rice, or just some good old chicken wings, with *Slow Cooker Favorites: Chicken* you'll always know what's for dinner.

CHAPTER 1

Slow Cooker Basics

So you know you want to use a slow cooker and you're excited to whip up the delicious chicken dishes found throughout the book. But, where do you start? In this chapter, you'll learn everything you need to know to choose, cook with, clean, and store your slow cooker. In addition, you'll find some basic techniques for using this appliance as well as some info on the methods and terminology used in the book to make cooking with your slow cooker as easy as possible. Let's get cooking!

What Slow Cooker Equipment Should You Buy?

Maybe you've gone to buy a slow cooker and were intimidated by all the options. It can be intimidating. With so many different styles from which to choose, how do you pick the one that's right for you?

There are small 1-quart versions that are perfect for hot-dip appetizers and large 8-quart models that make enough stew for a large family. There are versions with automatic timers and warming settings. Some have removable crockery inserts, while others have the crock built into the device.

The first thing you need to do is take a look at how you'll be using the device. Are you routinely gone for more than nine hours during the day? If so, you might want to consider the automatic timer and warming function because even a slow cooker can overcook some food. Do you want to make entire meals? The two-compartment model would provide more options. If you don't like to spend a lot of time washing pots and pans, consider a slow cooker with a removable crockery insert. These can be cleaned in the dishwasher while self-contained units must be sponge cleaned. The good news is that a slow cooker remains a slow cooker. It's a relatively simple device that's hard to use incorrectly.

If you are lucky enough to plan your purchase of a slow cooker, define what you will be using it for. Do you have more than four people in your family? If so, you might want to go with a 6-quart or even 8-quart version. Someone who does a lot of entertaining or likes to freeze leftovers might want the larger version. Many of the recipes throughout this book call for either a 4- or a 6-quart slow cooker, so keep that in mind while choosing your appliance. Once you decide what type of slow cooker to buy, you'll need to figure out how to use it. Read on…

How to Use Your Slow Cooker

Today's slow cookers usually have two settings—high and low. The low setting is equivalent to about 200°F at its highest, while the high setting gets up to about 300°F. However, the reason they are listed as high and low is because the actual degrees don't matter. Since the food heats indirectly, absorbing the heat from the crockery, it will cook the same way within a 50-degree temperature range.

Slow cookers heat up slowly, usually taking two to three hours to get up to their highest temperature. This ensures that the food retains its nutrients while also preventing scorching or burning. It's also the reason you don't need to be home while the meal cooks. When your slow cooker is on, resist the urge to lift the cover to view, smell, or stir the contents. Every time you lift the cover of the slow cooker, valuable steam escapes, reducing the internal temperature several degrees. This steam that the slow cooker creates is an important factor in creating those marvelous flavors—foods are cooked in their own steam, literally infusing the flavor back in through the cooking process. This keeps the food moist and works to tenderize the chicken and even the most stubborn vegetables. Every time you lift the cover, plan to add at least twenty minutes to your cooking time.

Slow Cooker Suggestions

The heating elements for a slow cooker are across the bottom of the slow cooker and up the sides. Until you become very familiar with the quirks of your slow cooker, cooking on low is the safest bet for ensuring the food turns out the way you want it.

Even the most inexperienced cook can quickly master slow cooker recipes. Just keep the following things in mind:

- Cut chicken and vegetables to the same size to ensure even cooking in soups and stews.
- Place slow-cooking items such as hard vegetables—rutabagas, turnips, potatoes—on the bottom of the slow cooker.
- Slow cooker recipes don't like water. Because the food is infused with steam, very little water escapes. When converting a recipe from a regular cookbook, use about half the water and add more during the last hour of the cooking cycle if necessary.

- Most traditional slow cooker recipes take seven to nine hours on the low setting. The high setting takes about half that time but doesn't tenderize the chicken as much.
- Spices and aromatic vegetables have different characteristics when slow cooked. Some, such as green peppers and bay leaves, increase in intensity when slow cooked. Others, such as onions and cinnamon, tend to lose flavor over the long cooking process. Most slow cooker recipes reflect this difference, although you may have to adjust for your own tastes.
- When cooking traditional slow cooker meals such as soups, stews, and meats, make sure the slow cooker is at least half full and the food does not extend beyond 1" below the top. This ensures even cooking.
- Don't thaw food in the slow cooker. While it may seem a natural use, frozen food actually heats up too slowly to effectively prevent bacterial growth when in a slow cooker. It's better to thaw food overnight in a refrigerator or use the microwave.

With these things in mind, you'll be a slow cooker professional before you know it.

How to Care for Your Slow Cooker

Slow cookers are very simple appliances. However, they do need some special care. If you follow these rules your slow cooker will produce healthy meals for many years:

- Never, never, never immerse the slow cooker in water. If it's plugged in at the time, you could receive a shock. If it isn't plugged in, you could damage the heating element.
- Always check for nicks or cuts in the electrical cord before plugging it into the outlet. This is especially important because you may be leaving the slow cooker on for several hours with no one in the house.
- Parts of the slow cooker can be cleaned in a dishwasher. If you have a removable crockery core, place it on the bottom rack. If you have a

plastic cover, be sure to place it in the top rack of the dishwasher so it doesn't warp. If the crockery container isn't removable, simply use a soft cloth or sponge to wash it out. Always use a damp cloth to wash the metal housing.

- Remove baked-on food from the crockery container with a nonabrasive cleaner and a damp sponge. Do not scrub with abrasives, as these can scratch the crock, creating areas for bacteria to reside.

Be sure to follow all of these rules to guarantee your slow cooker will both last for many years and perform at maximum potential with each use.

Slow Cooker Suggestions

Cooking with a slow cooker becomes even easier when you use slow cooker liners. The liners are made of food-safe, heat-resistant nylon. They also make slow cooker cleanup fast and easy, because you simply place the liner in the slow cooker crock, add the ingredients, cook according to the recipe instructions, throw the liner away when you're done, and wipe down the slow cooker and wash the lid.

What Else Do You Need to Know?

So now you know how to buy, cook with, and clean your slow cooker. Now let's take a look at what else you need to know to successfully make the deliciously easy meals found throughout the following chapters.

Learn Some Cooking Terms

Throughout this book, you'll encounter cooking terms usually associated with other methods of cooking. While the slow cooker does provide an easy way to cook foods, there are simple tricks you can use to let your slow cooker mimic those other methods. Cooking method terms you'll find in this book include the following:

- **Baking** usually involves putting the food that's in a baking pan or ovenproof casserole dish in a preheated oven; the food cooks by being surrounded by the hot, dry air of your oven. (In the case of a convection oven, it cooks by being surrounded by circulating hot, dry air.) In the slow cooker, food can be steam-baked in the cooker itself, or you can mimic the effect of baking at a low oven temperature by putting the food in a baking dish and resting that dish on a cooking insert or rack.

- **Braising** usually starts by browning chicken in a skillet on top of the stove and then putting the chicken with a small amount of liquid in a pan with a lid or covering and slowly cooking it. Braising can take place on the stovetop, in the oven, or in a slow cooker. The slow-cooking process tenderizes the chicken. Incidentally, the liquid that's in the pan after you've braised chicken often can be used to make a flavorful sauce or gravy.

- **Sautéing** is the method of quickly cooking small or thin pieces of food in some oil or butter that has been brought to temperature in a sauté pan over medium to medium-high heat. Alternatively, you can sauté in a good-quality nonstick pan without using added fat; instead use a little broth, nonstick cooking spray, or water in place of the oil or butter. As mentioned later in this chapter, another alternative is to steam-sauté food in the microwave.

- **Stewing** is similar to braising in that food is slowly cooked in a liquid; however, stewing involves a larger liquid-to-food ratio. In other words, you use far more liquid when you're stewing food. It is the method often associated with recipes for the slow cooker. Not surprisingly, this method is most often used to make stew.

Make Each Dish Your Own

Throughout this book you'll find suggestions for how you can take shortcuts or add a bit of additional personality to a dish without compromising the recipe. Straying from the recipe may seem scary at first, but once you understand the logic behind such shortcuts, you'll begin to look at them as alternative measures rather than total improvisations. Before you know it, you'll be adding a little bit of this and a little bit of that with the best of them. For example:

- **Use broth bases or homemade broth:** Use of a broth base or homemade broth lets you eliminate the need to stir-fry chicken and sauté vegetables. In addition, broth bases can be made double strength, which saves you the time of reducing broth and you avoid that briny, overly salty taste associated with bouillon cubes. Bases also take up less storage space. It usually only takes ¾ to 1 teaspoon of broth mixed together with a cup of water to make 1 cup of broth. A 16-ounce container of base, for example, is enough to make 6 gallons of broth.

- **Use a microwave-safe measuring cup:** Rather than dirtying a microwave-safe bowl and a measuring cup, planning the steps so that you add the ingredients to a microwave-safe measuring cup means you can use it to sauté or steam onions or other vegetables called for in the recipe. This makes it easier to pour the results into the slow cooker and you end up with fewer dishes to wash.

- **Steam-sauté vegetables in the microwave:** Sautéing vegetables in the microwave has the added advantage of using less oil than it would take to sauté them in a pan. Or you can compromise further and eliminate the oil entirely and substitute broth if you prefer. Just because a recipe suggests sautéing the onions in a nonstick skillet doesn't mean that you can't use the alternative microwave method, or vice versa. Use the method that is most convenient for you. On the other hand, skipping other steps, like sautéing onion, carrot, celery, or bell pepper before you add them to the slow cooker, won't ruin the taste of the food; you'll just end up with a dish that tastes good instead of great. When time is an issue, there may be times when good is good enough. And that's okay.

- **Take advantage of ways to enhance or correct the flavor:** Like salt, a little bit of sugar can act as a flavor enhancer. The sweetness of sugar, honey, applesauce, or jelly can also be used to help tame an overly hot spicy dish or curry. Just start out adding a little bit at a time; you want to adjust the flavor without ending up with a dish with a cloying result.

- **Use fresh herbs:** There are other times you may need to adjust some of the recipe instructions. For example, if you have fresh herbs on hand, it's almost always better to use those instead of dried seasoning; however, if you substitute fresh herbs, don't add them until near the end of the cooking time. Also keep in mind that you need to use three times the amount called for in the recipe. In other words, if the recipe specifies 1 teaspoon of dried thyme, you'd add 1 tablespoon (3 teaspoons) of fresh thyme.

- **Use frozen, not fresh:** If you're using frozen meat to replace the raw meat called for in the recipe, chances are you can add it straight from the freezer to the slow cooker and not greatly affect the cooking time. If the meat is thawed, you'll want to wait until near the end of the cooking time to add it so that you don't overcook the meat.

Again, if you're nervous or just aren't comfortable cooking with a slow cooker yet, don't worry. Follow the recipes throughout the book, learn what you like and what you don't like, and then take the next step. The possibilities are endless!

CHAPTER 2

Easy Essential Chicken Recipes

18 Chicken Stock

19 Chicken Broth

20 "Precooked" Chicken

20 Poached Chicken

21 Rotisserie-Style Chicken

22 Roast Chicken

22 Foolproof Chicken

23 Chicken Braised in Beer

23 Steamed Chicken Sandwich

24 Spicy Plum Chicken

25 Mushroom Chicken Breast

26 Chicken in Onion-Mushroom Gravy

27 Spiced Apple Cider Chicken

27 Spicy Roasted Chicken Breast

28 Wild Rice–Stuffed Chicken Breast Cutlets

29 Chicken and Gherkin Sandwich

29 Ground Chicken and Carrot Quiche

Chicken Stock

YIELDS

3 QT

1 chicken carcass

2 carrots, cut into chunks

2 celery stalks, cut into chunks

2 onions, peeled and cut into chunks

2 parsnips, cut into chunks

1 head garlic

2 chicken wings

Water, as needed

1. Place the carcass, carrots, celery, onions, parsnips, garlic, and wings into a 6-quart slow cooker.

2. Fill the slow cooker with water until it is 2" below the top. Cover and cook on low for 10 hours.

3. Strain into a large container. Discard the solids. Refrigerate the stock overnight.

4. The next day, scoop off any fat that has floated to the top. Discard the fat.

5. Freeze or refrigerate the broth until ready to use.

Slow Cooker Suggestions

Any leftover vegetables can be added to stock for extra flavor; fennel fronds, green onions, turnips, and red onion are all good choices. Depending on the recipe that the stock will be used in, adding items like dried chilies, ginger, or galangal root will customize the stock, making it an even better fit for the final product.

Chicken Broth

3 pounds bone-in chicken pieces

1 large onion, peeled and quartered

2 large carrots, scrubbed

2 celery stalks

1 teaspoon salt

½ teaspoon freshly ground black pepper

4½ cups water

1. Add the chicken pieces and onion to a 4- to 6-quart slow cooker.
2. Slice the carrots and cut the celery into pieces that will fit in the slow cooker and add them. Add the salt, pepper, and water. Cover and cook on low for 6–8 hours. (Cooking time will depend on the size of the chicken pieces.) Allow to cool to room temperature.
3. Strain, discarding the cooked vegetables. Remove any meat from the chicken bones and save for another use. Refrigerate the (cooled) broth overnight. Remove and discard the hardened fat. The resulting concentrated broth can be kept for 1 week in the refrigerator or frozen for up to 3 months.

Slow Cooker Suggestions

The chicken fat that will rise to the top of the broth and harden overnight in the refrigerator is known as schmaltz. You can save that fat and use it instead of butter for sautéing vegetables.

"Precooked" Chicken

4 large skinless, boneless chicken breasts
½ cup Chicken Broth (see recipe in this chapter)

1. Place chicken breasts in a greased 4-quart slow cooker. Pour Chicken Broth over the chicken.
2. Cook on high for 3–4 hours or on low for 6–7 hours.
3. Place chicken and broth in the refrigerator for up to 3 days until needed. Do not cut chicken until it's completely cooled, to help retain its moisture. If not used within 3 days, freeze for up to a month.

Slow Cooker Suggestions

Use this chicken for quick weeknight stir-fries or chicken salad. It can also be added to pasta dishes or served with baked potatoes and steamed broccoli.

Poached Chicken

4½ pounds whole chicken
1 carrot, peeled and cut into chunks

1 celery stalk, cut into chunks
1 onion, peeled and quartered
1 cup water

1. Place the chicken into an oval 6-quart slow cooker. Arrange the vegetables around the chicken. Add the water. Cook on low for 7–8 hours.
2. Remove the skin before eating.

Slow Cooker Suggestions

Stir together 2 cups cubed poached chicken breast, 3 tablespoons mayonnaise, ¼ cup diced celery, 1 minced shallot, and ¼ cup dried cranberries. Refrigerate for 1 hour. Serve on multigrain crackers or whole-wheat rolls.

Rotisserie-Style Chicken

1 (4-pound) whole chicken

1½ teaspoons salt

2 teaspoons paprika

½ teaspoon onion powder

½ teaspoon dried thyme

½ teaspoon dried basil

½ teaspoon ground white pepper

½ teaspoon ground cayenne powder

½ teaspoon ground black pepper

½ teaspoon garlic powder

2 tablespoons olive oil

1. Rinse the chicken in cold water and pat dry with a paper towel.

2. In a small bowl mix together salt, paprika, onion powder, thyme, basil, white pepper, cayenne powder, black pepper, and garlic powder.

3. Rub the spice mixture over the entire chicken. Rub part of the spice mixture underneath the skin, making sure to leave the skin intact.

4. Place the spice-rubbed chicken in a greased 6-quart slow cooker. Drizzle olive oil evenly over the chicken. Cook on high for 3–3½ hours or on low for 4–5 hours.

5. Remove chicken carefully from the slow cooker and place on a large plate or serving platter.

Slow Cooker Suggestions

If you would like to make a gravy to go with the chicken, follow these directions: After removing the cooked chicken, turn slow cooker on high. Whisk ⅓ cup garbanzo bean flour or ⅓ cup brown rice flour into the cooking juices. Add ¼ teaspoon salt and ¼ teaspoon pepper and cook for 10–15 minutes, whisking occasionally, until sauce has thickened. Spoon gravy over chicken.

Roast Chicken

4 medium white potatoes, quartered

1 small onion, peeled and quartered

2 carrots, peeled and sliced

1 large celery stalk, sliced

1 (3½-pound) whole chicken

2 tablespoons olive oil

1 teaspoon salt

½ teaspoon ground black pepper

½ teaspoon dried thyme

¼ teaspoon dried rosemary

1. Add potatoes, onion, carrots, and celery to the bottom of a greased 4-quart slow cooker.
2. Rinse off whole chicken, pat dry with a paper towel, and place on top of the vegetables.
3. Drizzle chicken with olive oil. Sprinkle salt, pepper, and herbs evenly over chicken.
4. Cover and cook on high for 3½ hours or on low for 6 hours.

Foolproof Chicken

3 pounds boneless, skinless chicken breast

3 (8-ounce) cans tomato sauce

Place chicken in a 4-quart slow cooker and add sauce. Cover and cook on low for 8 hours or on high for 4–5 hours. Once cooked, shred the chicken with a fork and enjoy.

Chicken Braised in Beer

SERVES 6

3 boneless, skinless chicken breasts

1 onion, peeled and quartered

6 ounces beer

1½ cups water

2 cloves garlic

1. Place all ingredients in a 4-quart slow cooker. Cook on low for 6 hours.
2. Remove the chicken breasts and discard the cooking liquid.

Steamed Chicken Sandwich

SERVES 6

12 slices bacon

12 slices sourdough bread

3 tomatoes

½ pound chicken, cooked

½ pound Cheddar cheese

2 tablespoons butter

2 teaspoons mustard

1. Sauté the bacon in a pan over medium heat until crispy; drain.
2. Toast the bread; slice the tomatoes. Thinly slice the chicken and the cheese.
3. Arrange the sandwich layers in this order: bread, butter, chicken, cheese, bacon, tomato, mustard, butter, bread.
4. Wrap the sandwiches in foil and arrange on a trivet in the slow cooker. Pour water around the base of the trivet.
5. Cover and heat on a high setting for 1–2 hours.

Spicy Plum Chicken

2 pounds boneless chicken

½ teaspoon ground white pepper

½ teaspoon ground ginger

½ teaspoon ground cinnamon

¼ teaspoon ground cloves

4 tablespoons soy sauce, divided

2 tablespoons honey

½ cup plum jelly

2 teaspoons sugar

2 teaspoons vinegar

¼ cup chutney

1. Cut the chicken into serving-sized pieces. Mix the spices and divide the spice mixture in half. Sprinkle the chicken with half of this mixture.

2. To the other half of the spice mixture, add 1 tablespoon soy sauce. Sprinkle this over the chicken, as well. Refrigerate the chicken for 4 hours or overnight.

3. Arrange the chicken pieces in the slow cooker.

4. Mix the remaining 3 tablespoons of soy sauce with the honey, jelly, sugar, vinegar, and chutney. Dribble this mixture over the chicken pieces in the slow cooker.

5. Cover and heat on a low setting for 3–4 hours.

Mushroom Chicken Breast

1 teaspoon butter

1 medium onion, peeled and sliced

8 ounces cremini mushrooms, cleaned and sliced

1½ pounds chicken breast cutlets

1 teaspoon minced fresh sage leaves

⅛ teaspoon salt

¼ teaspoon ground black pepper

¼ cup water

1. Heat the butter in a nonstick skillet. Add the onions and mushrooms and sauté until the onions are beginning to soften. Add half of the onion and mushroom mixture to a 4-quart slow cooker. Add the chicken. Sprinkle with sage, salt, and pepper. Top with the remaining onion and mushroom mixture.

2. Add the water. Cook on high for 2–3 hours or on low for 6–8 hours.

Slow Cooker Suggestions

Make sure that your slow cooker is at least half filled before cooking for best results. If the slow cooker is not filled halfway, the food will cook too quickly and might burn or dry out. Aim for half to two-thirds of the way full.

Chicken in Onion-Mushroom Gravy

SERVES 8

Nonstick spray

½ cup water

3 pounds boneless chicken breast

1 envelope dry onion soup mix

1 small onion, peeled and thinly sliced

8 ounces fresh mushrooms, cleaned and sliced

8 medium red potatoes, peeled

1 tablespoon butter, softened

1 tablespoon all-purpose flour

1 cup heavy cream

¼ teaspoon salt

¼ teaspoon freshly ground black pepper

1. Treat the crock of the slow cooker with nonstick spray. Add the water. Place the chicken in the slow cooker and sprinkle the soup mix over the top of it. Add the onion, mushrooms, and potatoes. Cover and cook on low for 8 hours or until the chicken reaches an internal temperature of 170°F.

2. Move the chicken breast and potatoes to a serving platter; cover and keep warm.

3. Cover, increase the slow cooker to high, and cook for 15 minutes or until the liquid in the crock is bubbling around the edges. Mix the butter and flour together; dollop into the cooker. Whisk to work into the liquid, stirring and cooking for 5 minutes or until the flour taste is cooked out of the sauce and the mixture begins to thicken. Whisk in the cream and continue to cook for 15 minutes or until the cream comes to temperature and the gravy coats the back of a spoon. Season with salt and pepper.

4. Slice the chicken and ladle the gravy over the slices, and serve the extra on the side.

Slow Cooker Suggestions

Omit the potatoes and cook the Chicken in Onion-Mushroom Gravy recipe as directed through Step 2. Stir 1 cup of sour cream into the liquid in the slow cooker, continuing to cook and stir until the mixture comes to temperature. Serve over cooked egg noodles and the sliced chicken.

Spiced Apple Cider Chicken

Nonstick spray

3 pounds boneless chicken breast

¼ teaspoon salt

¼ teaspoon freshly ground black pepper

2 apples

4 large sweet potatoes

½ cup apple cider

½ teaspoon ground cinnamon

¼ teaspoon ground cloves

¼ teaspoon ground allspice

2 tablespoons brown sugar

1. Treat the crock of the slow cooker with nonstick spray. Add chicken breast and season it with salt and pepper.

2. Peel, core, and slice the apples; arrange the slices over and around the chicken.

3. Peel the sweet potatoes and cut each in half; add to the slow cooker.

4. Add the cider, cinnamon, cloves, allspice, and brown sugar to a bowl or measuring cup; stir to combine and pour over the ingredients in the slow cooker.

5. Cover and cook on low for 8 hours or until the internal temperature of the chicken is 170°F.

Spicy Roasted Chicken Breast

2 teaspoons ground cayenne powder

2 teaspoons ground chipotle powder

2 teaspoons freshly ground black pepper

½ teaspoon salt

2½ pounds bone-in chicken breast

2 jalapeño peppers, minced

1 teaspoon hot sauce

¾ cup water

1. Rub the dry spices into the chicken breast. Place into an oval 4-quart slow cooker. Top with jalapeños, hot sauce, and water.

2. Cook on low for 8 hours or until fully cooked. Remove the skin before serving.

Wild Rice–Stuffed Chicken Breast Cutlets

SERVES
4

1 onion, peeled and sliced

4 ounces button mushrooms, cleaned and sliced

1 cup cooked wild rice

1 tablespoon minced fresh parsley leaves

1 teaspoon fresh thyme leaves

½ tablespoon finely minced fresh basil leaves

1 teaspoon minced fresh rosemary leaves

¼ teaspoon ground black pepper

2 cloves garlic, peeled and minced

4 chicken breast cutlets (about 1 pound)

½ cup Chicken Stock (see recipe in this chapter)

1. Place the onion and mushrooms on the bottom of a 4-quart slow cooker.
2. In a large bowl, mix together the wild rice, parsley, thyme, basil, rosemary, black pepper, and garlic. Divide the rice mixture into 4 portions. Place a single portion in the center of each chicken cutlet. Roll, rice side in, and secure with a toothpick or kitchen twine. Place on top of the onions and mushrooms in the slow cooker. Pour the stock over the top.
3. Cook on low for 4 hours.

Chicken and Gherkin Sandwich

12 slices rye bread	2 tablespoons butter
½ pound cooked chicken	½ teaspoon salt
6 baby dill pickles	½ teaspoon ground black pepper
¼ pound mozzarella cheese	

1. Toast the bread on one side. Thinly slice the chicken, pickles, and cheese.
2. Arrange the sandwich layers in this order: bread (toasted side out), butter, chicken, salt, pepper, pickle, cheese, butter, bread.
3. Wrap the sandwiches in foil and arrange on a trivet in the slow cooker. Pour water around the base of the trivet.
4. Cover and heat on a high setting for 1–2 hours.

Ground Chicken and Carrot Quiche

6 large eggs	5 tablespoons coconut milk
½ pound ground chicken, browned	4 tablespoons minced fresh parsley leaves
1 cup shredded carrots	½ teaspoon coriander powder
½ cup Chicken Broth (see recipe in this chapter)	Coconut oil, for greasing slow cooker

1. Crack the eggs into a medium bowl and beat well with a wire whisk.
2. Add the chicken, carrots, and all remaining ingredients except coconut oil, and stir.
3. Grease bottom and sides of a 2- to 4-quart slow cooker with coconut oil. Add the egg mixture to the slow cooker, cover, and cook on low for 1 hour.
4. Stir the eggs with a fork to help break them up for even cooking. Cover, and cook on low for 1 hour. Fluff with a fork and serve warm.

CHAPTER 3

Appetizers

32 Stuffed Grape Leaves

33 Hot Chicken Buffalo Bites

33 Chicken Bites

34 Honey Mustard Chicken Fingers

35 Chicken Meatballs in a Hawaiian-Inspired Sauce

36 Light and Creamy Swedish Meatballs

37 Coconut Chicken Fingers

38 Curried Chicken Meatballs with Tomatoes

39 Curried Chicken Dip

40 Ground Chicken Tomato Sauce

41 Chicken Chowder

41 Chicken Tetrazzini

42 Spicy Buffalo Nuggets with Ranch Dressing

Stuffed Grape Leaves

16 ounces jarred grape leaves (about 60 leaves)

Cooking spray, as needed

¾ pound ground chicken

1 shallot, peeled and minced

¾ cup cooked white rice

¼ cup minced fresh dill

½ cup lemon juice, divided

2 tablespoons minced fresh parsley leaves

1 tablespoon dried mint

1 tablespoon ground fennel

¼ teaspoon freshly ground black pepper

⅛ teaspoon salt

2 cups water

1. Prepare the grape leaves according to package instructions. Set aside.

2. Spray a nonstick skillet with cooking spray. Sauté the meat and shallot until the meat is thoroughly cooked. Drain off any excess fat. Scrape into a bowl and add the rice, dill, ¼ cup of the lemon juice, parsley, mint, fennel, pepper, and salt. Stir to incorporate all ingredients.

3. Place a leaf, stem side up, with the top of the leaf pointing away from you on a clean work surface. Place 1 teaspoon filling in the middle of the leaf. Fold the bottom toward the middle and then fold in the sides. Roll it toward the top to seal. Repeat.

4. Place the rolled grape leaves in 2 or 3 layers in a 4-quart oval slow cooker. Pour in the water and remaining lemon juice. Cover and cook on low for 4–6 hours. Serve warm or cold.

Slow Cooker Suggestions

Here's a simple Greek-style dipping sauce recipe that goes great with these Stuffed Grape Leaves: In a medium bowl, stir together 1 cup fat-free Greek yogurt and 1 teaspoon each dried oregano, mint, thyme, dill weed, and white pepper. Stir in 3 tablespoons lemon juice. Refrigerate 1 hour before serving. Refrigerate leftovers in an airtight container.

Hot Chicken Buffalo Bites

SERVES
6

3 large chicken breasts, cut into 2" strips

2 tablespoons brown rice flour

¼ cup melted butter

3 cloves garlic, peeled and minced

⅓ cup Frank's RedHot sauce

¼ cup gluten-free ranch dressing

1. Place chicken pieces into a greased 2.5-quart slow cooker.
2. In a saucepan whisk together the brown rice flour and melted butter for 2–3 minutes to toast the flour.
3. Slowly whisk in the garlic and Frank's RedHot sauce. Pour sauce over chicken in the slow cooker.
4. Cover and cook on high for 3 hours or on low for 6 hours. Serve with ranch dressing to dip in. If using a larger slow cooker, make sure to reduce cooking time by about half.

Chicken Bites

SERVES
16

2 pounds boneless skinless chicken breast, cubed

1 onion, peeled and minced

2 cloves garlic, peeled and minced

½ cup chili sauce

½ cup no-sugar raspberry jam

1 tablespoon Worcestershire sauce

1 tablespoon balsamic vinegar

1. Place the chicken into a 4-quart slow cooker. In a small bowl, whisk together the onion, garlic, chili sauce, jam, Worcestershire sauce, and balsamic vinegar. Pour it over the meat.
2. Cook on low for 3 hours or until the chicken is cooked through. Stir before serving.

Honey Mustard Chicken Fingers

4 large boneless, skinless chicken breasts, patted dry and
   cut into strips

1 egg, beaten

1½ cups blanched almond flour

Nonstick spray or olive oil

⅓ cup honey

⅓ cup Dijon mustard

1 teaspoon dried basil

1 teaspoon paprika

½ teaspoon salt

½ teaspoon ground black pepper

½ teaspoon dried parsley

1. Dip chicken strips into the egg and dredge through the blanched almond flour.

2. Using nonstick spray or olive oil, brown chicken strips in a skillet in small batches just until they are golden brown, approximately 1 minute per side.

3. Make a 2"–3" foil rack in the bottom of your 4-quart slow cooker by placing rolled strips of aluminum foil in the bottom of the greased insert. Make a grill pattern with the strips. This will allow the chicken to cook above the juices while sitting on the rack.

4. In a small bowl mix together the honey, mustard, basil, paprika, salt, pepper, and parsley.

5. Place browned chicken fingers on the rack in the slow cooker. Drizzle half of the honey mustard sauce evenly over the chicken. Cook on high for 3 hours or on low for 6 hours. Serve the chicken tenders with the remaining honey mustard sauce.

Chicken Meatballs in a Hawaiian-Inspired Sauce

2 pounds ground chicken breast

1 teaspoon ground ginger

2 tablespoons plus ¾ cup pineapple juice, divided

½ cup bread crumbs

1 egg

¼ cup minced onion

2 cloves garlic, peeled and grated

¼ cup soy sauce

¼ cup teriyaki sauce

¼ cup ponzu sauce

3 tablespoons lime juice

1 tablespoon cornstarch

½ tablespoon peeled and grated fresh ginger

1 small onion, peeled and thinly sliced

4 cups cubed fresh pineapple

1 jalapeño pepper, minced

⅓ cup brown sugar

1. Preheat the oven to 375°F. Line 2 baking sheets with parchment paper. In a large bowl, use your hands to mix the chicken, ground ginger, 2 tablespoons of pineapple juice, bread crumbs, egg, minced onion, and garlic. Form into 1" balls. Place on the baking sheets and bake for 15 minutes or until cooked through.

2. Meanwhile, in a small bowl, whisk together the remaining pineapple juice, soy sauce, teriyaki sauce, ponzu sauce, lime juice, and cornstarch. Pour into a 6-quart slow cooker.

3. Add the grated ginger, sliced onion, pineapple, jalapeño, and brown sugar to the slow cooker. Stir.

4. Add the meatballs and cook on low for 6–9 hours.

Slow Cooker Suggestions

Cut ½" off the bottom and top of the pineapple. Use a knife to slice off the skin and remove any "eyes." Slice the flesh from around the round core. Discard the core and cube the flesh.

Light and Creamy Swedish Meatballs

SERVES
20

2 thin slices white sandwich bread

½ cup 1% milk

2 pounds ground chicken

2 cloves garlic, peeled and minced

1 egg

½ teaspoon ground allspice, divided

¼ teaspoon ground nutmeg, divided

3 cups Chicken Stock (see recipe in Chapter 2)

1 (12-ounce) can fat-free evaporated milk

1 tablespoon melted butter

⅓ cup all-purpose flour

1. Preheat oven to 350°F. In a shallow saucepan, cook the bread and milk on low heat until the milk is absorbed, about 1 minute. Place the bread into a large bowl and add the chicken, garlic, egg, ¼ teaspoon allspice, and ⅛ teaspoon nutmeg.

2. Mix until all ingredients are evenly distributed. Roll into 1" balls. Line 2 baking sheets with parchment paper. Place the meatballs in a single layer on the baking sheets. Bake for 15 minutes, and then drain on paper towel–lined plates.

3. Meanwhile, bring the stock, evaporated milk, butter, and remaining nutmeg and allspice to a simmer. Whisk in the flour and continue to whisk until the mixture is slightly thickened. Remove from heat.

4. Place the meatballs into a 4- or 6-quart oval slow cooker. Pour the sauce over the meatballs. Cook on low up to 6 hours. Stir gently before serving to distribute the sauce evenly.

Coconut Chicken Fingers

Cooking spray

3 tablespoons fresh lemon juice

3 tablespoons fresh lime juice

3 tablespoons spicy brown mustard

½ cup plain toasted bread crumbs

½ cup unsweetened shredded coconut

½ teaspoon kosher salt

¼ teaspoon ground black pepper

¼ teaspoon curry powder

¼ teaspoon dried oregano

4 skinless, boneless chicken breasts, cut into 2" × 1" strips

¼ cup (½ stick) margarine, melted

Honey Mustard Dipping Sauce (see recipe in sidebar)

1. Spray the inside of a 4-quart slow cooker with the cooking spray. Set aside.

2. In a small bowl, whisk together the lemon juice, lime juice, and the mustard.

3. In another bowl, combine the bread crumbs, coconut, salt, pepper, curry powder, and oregano.

4. Dip the chicken strips in the mustard mixture, followed by the bread crumb mixture. Place in the prepared slow cooker. Drizzle the melted margarine over the chicken.

5. Cover and cook on high for 2–4 hours, or until the chicken fingers are fully cooked. Serve with Honey Mustard Dipping Sauce alongside.

Slow Cooker Suggestions

To make Honey Mustard Dipping Sauce, whisk together 3 tablespoons spicy brown mustard, 2 tablespoons honey, and 3 tablespoons mayonnaise until smooth. Cover and refrigerate until ready to use. Makes approximately ½ cup.

Curried Chicken Meatballs with Tomatoes

SERVES

4

2 teaspoons plus 1 tablespoon olive oil, divided

2 slices toasted Italian bread

1 pound ground chicken

2 large eggs

1 small red onion, peeled and finely diced

1 small carrot, peeled and finely diced

1 teaspoon curry powder

1/2 teaspoon paprika

1/4 bunch flat-leaf parsley, chopped

1/2 teaspoon kosher salt

1/2 teaspoon freshly ground black pepper

1 (28-ounce) can crushed tomatoes

1. Grease a 4- to 5-quart slow cooker with 2 teaspoons olive oil.

2. Soak the bread in water to cover for 20 minutes, or until the bread has absorbed all of the moisture, and squeeze out by hand. Roughly chop the bread. In a large bowl, combine bread, chicken, eggs, onion, carrot, curry powder, paprika, parsley, salt, and pepper.

3. Form into 16 small meatballs. Heat remaining olive oil in a large skillet over medium heat until it shimmers, about 1 minute. Add meatballs and brown on all sides, about 8 minutes. Place meatballs in slow cooker and add tomatoes.

4. Cook on low for 6 hours.

Curried Chicken Dip

1 tablespoon olive oil

1 pound boneless, skinless chicken breast, diced in ½" pieces

½ teaspoon kosher salt

1 teaspoon freshly ground black pepper

1 large carrot, peeled and diced

1 large red onion, peeled and diced

1 shallot, peeled and diced

1 clove garlic, peeled and minced

2 tablespoons curry powder

¼ teaspoon red pepper flakes

½ cup Chicken Broth (see recipe in Chapter 2)

½ cup chopped fresh spinach leaves

½ cup low-fat Greek yogurt

2 teaspoons lemon juice

1. Heat olive oil in a large skillet over medium heat. Add chicken and season with salt and pepper. Sauté over medium heat for 2 minutes.

2. Add the carrot, onion, and shallot and cook for 5–7 minutes until softened. Add garlic, curry powder, and red pepper flakes and cook for 1 minute, stirring well. Place the chicken mixture in a 4- to 5-quart slow cooker with the Chicken Broth. Heat on low for 3½ hours.

3. Add the spinach, yogurt, and lemon juice and stir well. Cook for an additional hour.

Slow Cooker Suggestions

One of the main ingredients in curry is turmeric, and not only does it add a lovely golden color to the spice mixture, it also adds an unexpected health benefit. Turmeric's active compound, curcumin, prevents sharp spikes in blood sugar. It's also an anti-inflammatory agent.

Ground Chicken Tomato Sauce

2 tablespoons olive oil

1 pound ground chicken

1 (14.5-ounce) can stewed tomatoes

1 (6-ounce) can tomato paste

½ teaspoon dried thyme

1 teaspoon dried basil

½ teaspoon dried oregano

1 teaspoon honey

1 yellow onion, peeled and chopped

1 green bell pepper, chopped

2 cloves garlic, peeled and crushed

1 bay leaf

¼ cup water

4 ounces chopped mushrooms, fresh (cleaned)

1. Heat the olive oil in a skillet over medium heat. Add the ground chicken and cook for 5–7 minutes until brown.
2. While browning chicken, place stewed tomatoes, tomato paste, thyme, basil, oregano, and honey in a 4- to 6-quart slow cooker. Stir well and turn slow cooker to low heat.
3. Next, transfer browned chicken to the slow cooker with a slotted spoon. In the pan with ground chicken drippings, sauté the onion, pepper, garlic, and bay leaf for 3–5 minutes until softened.
4. To the slow cooker, add the sautéed vegetables, water, and the chopped mushrooms. Cover and cook on low 4–6 hours. Thin with a little water if necessary.

Chicken Chowder

1 pound skinless, boneless chicken thighs, cut into chunks

1 (14.5-ounce) can diced tomatoes

1 (8-ounce) package of fresh, sliced mushrooms

1 large red onion, peeled and minced

6 cloves garlic, peeled and minced

½ cup Chicken Stock (see recipe in Chapter 2)

½ cup dry red wine

1 teaspoon dried oregano

1 teaspoon dried basil

1 teaspoon ground black pepper

1. Place all ingredients into a 4-quart slow cooker.
2. Cover and cook on low for 6 hours, stirring occasionally.

Chicken Tetrazzini

1 medium onion, peeled and diced

2 tablespoons unbleached flour

3 skinless, boneless chicken breasts, cut into 1" cubes

½ pound white button mushrooms, cleaned and sliced

1½ cups Chicken Stock (see recipe in Chapter 2)

½ cup almond milk

1 pound uncooked spaghetti, broken in half

½ cup frozen peas, defrosted

1 teaspoon kosher salt

¼ teaspoon ground black pepper

1. In a 6-quart slow cooker, combine the onion, flour, and the chicken breasts. Top with the mushrooms and pour in the stock. Cover and cook on low for 4–6 hours.
2. Stir in the almond milk, spaghetti, peas, salt, and pepper. Cover and cook on high for 20–30 minutes or until the spaghetti is done.

Spicy Buffalo Nuggets with Ranch Dressing

½ stick (¼ cup) margarine, cut up

1 tablespoon hot sauce, such as Frank's RedHot Sauce

1 tablespoon white vinegar

1 teaspoon garlic powder

1 pound frozen fully cooked chicken nuggets, defrosted

Ranch Dressing

1 cup mayonnaise

½ cup sour cream

½ teaspoon salt

½ teaspoon ground black pepper

½ teaspoon garlic powder

1½ tablespoons dried parsley

1 tablespoon chopped fresh chives

1 teaspoon dried dill weed

¼ teaspoon sweet paprika

1 teaspoon lemon juice

½ teaspoon Worcestershire sauce

1. Place margarine in a small bowl and microwave for 30 seconds, or until almost melted. Remove from microwave and stir until melted completely.

2. Add the hot sauce, vinegar, and garlic powder; stir well.

3. In a 4-quart slow cooker, add about a third of the sauce. Arrange chicken nuggets over sauce. Pour remaining sauce over nuggets. Cover and cook on low for 1 hour.

4. While nuggets are cooking, make the ranch dressing. Stir mayonnaise and sour cream together until completely blended. Stir in remaining dressing ingredients. Chill for at least 30 minutes before serving.

5. Serve the chicken nuggets with the ranch dressing.

CHAPTER 4

Wings and Drumsticks

44 Sticky Honey Wings

44 Green Curry Wings

45 Buffalo Chicken Wings

45 Sassy and Sweet Chicken Wings

46 Tandoori Chicken Wings

47 Green Chutney Wings

47 Pineapple Teriyaki Drumsticks

48 Gluten-Free "Shake It and Bake It" Drumsticks

49 Honey-Glazed Chicken Drumsticks

50 Chicken Drumsticks with Gluten-Free Stuffing

Sticky Honey Wings

3 pounds chicken wings, tips removed

¼ cup honey

¼ cup low-sodium soy sauce

½ teaspoon freshly ground black pepper

2 tablespoons chili sauce

½ teaspoon garlic powder

1. Place the wings into an oval 4-quart slow cooker.
2. In a small bowl, whisk the honey, soy sauce, pepper, chili sauce, and garlic powder. Pour over the wings. Toss to coat with sauce.
3. Cook for 6–7 hours on low. Stir before serving.

Slow Cooker Suggestions

Chili sauce is a smooth, mild red sauce. A mixture of tomato purée and spices, it is most often used as a base for other sauces. Chili-garlic sauce is a mixture of coarsely ground chilies and garlic. It is robustly flavored and used frequently in soups, stir-fries, and dipping sauces.

Green Curry Wings

3 pounds chicken wings, tips removed

8 ounces green curry paste

2 ounces fresh Thai basil leaves, minced

1 tablespoon light coconut milk

1 tablespoon peeled and minced fresh ginger

1 tablespoon minced fresh cilantro leaves

1. Place the wings into a 4-quart oval slow cooker.
2. In a small bowl, whisk together the curry paste, basil, coconut milk, ginger, and cilantro. Pour the sauce over the wings. Toss the wings to coat.
3. Cook on low for 6 hours. Stir prior to serving.

Buffalo Chicken Wings

SERVES **12**

4 tablespoons canola oil

4 tablespoons hot pepper sauce

1 tablespoon lime juice

¼ teaspoon ground black pepper

4 pounds chicken wings with wing tips removed, cut in half

1. Add oil, hot pepper sauce, and lime juice to a 4- to 6-quart slow cooker. Cook on high, about 15–20 minutes.
2. Add pepper to wings and broil in the oven until lightly browned, about 5–6 minutes on each side.
3. Add chicken wings to slow cooker, and stir to coat with the sauce. Cover and cook on high for 3–4 hours.

Slow Cooker Suggestions

For the boneless version of this classic appetizer, replace wings with 4 pounds of boneless, skinless tenders. Be prepared to eat with a fork! Serve as an appetizer as is, or on top of a bed of salad greens.

Sassy and Sweet Chicken Wings

SERVES **12**

4 pounds chicken wings

2 cups Brooks Rich & Tangy Ketchup

1 (12-ounce) can Coca-Cola

Add the chicken wings and ketchup to the slow cooker in alternating layers. Pour the cola over the chicken and ketchup. Cover and cook on low for 6–8 hours. Uncover and continue to cook on low until sauce is thickened. To serve, reduce the heat setting of the slow cooker to warm.

Slow Cooker Suggestions

An alternative to using Brooks Rich & Tangy Ketchup is to substitute 1 cup of regular ketchup and 1 cup of chili sauce.

Tandoori Chicken Wings

4 pounds chicken wings

¼ teaspoon salt

1 teaspoon ground black pepper

1½ tablespoons ginger-garlic paste

1 tablespoon tandoori masala

¼ cup thick hung yogurt

2 tablespoons lemon juice

1 tablespoon brown sugar

1. Place chicken wings in a bowl, and add salt and pepper. Mix. Place on a baking sheet and broil in the oven for 5–7 minutes on each side or until browned.

2. Take the chicken out of the oven; add the ginger-garlic paste and tandoori masala. Transfer it into a 6-quart slow cooker and cook on high for 2 hours, or on low for 4–5 hours, or until the chicken is cooked through.

3. In a small bowl, mix together the yogurt, lemon juice, and brown sugar. Around a half hour before the cooking time is over, pour in the yogurt mixture. Spread the coating all over the chicken wings. Cook for another 30 minutes.

4. Remove the chicken from the slow cooker. Pour the remaining liquid into a saucepan and reduce it over medium heat. Use it to coat the chicken before serving it hot.

Green Chutney Wings

3 pounds chicken wings, tips removed

8 ounces thick coriander chutney

3 tablespoons olive oil

1 tablespoon light coconut milk

1 tablespoon peeled and minced fresh ginger

¼ teaspoon salt

1. Place the wings into a 4-quart slow cooker.
2. Drain any extra liquid from the chutney. Chutney should be thick like a paste. In a small bowl, whisk together the chutney, oil, coconut milk, ginger, and salt. Pour the sauce over the wings. Toss the wings to coat.
3. Cook on low for 6 hours. Stir prior to serving.

Pineapple Teriyaki Drumsticks

12 chicken drumsticks

1 (8-ounce) can pineapple slices in juice

¼ cup low-sodium teriyaki sauce

1 teaspoon ground ginger

¼ cup hoisin sauce

1. Arrange the drumsticks in a single layer on a broiling pan. Broil in the oven for 10 minutes, flipping the drumsticks once halfway through the cooking time.
2. Drain the juice from the pineapple into a 4- or 6-quart oval slow cooker. Add the teriyaki sauce, ginger, and hoisin sauce. Stir to combine.
3. Cut the pineapple rings in half. Add them to the slow cooker.
4. Add the drumsticks to the slow cooker and stir to combine. Cover and cook on low for 4–6 hours.

Gluten-Free "Shake It and Bake It" Drumsticks

1 cup finely crushed gluten-free corn tortilla chips

1½ tablespoons olive oil

½ teaspoon salt

½ teaspoon paprika

¼ teaspoon celery seeds

¼ teaspoon ground black pepper

¼ teaspoon garlic powder

½ teaspoon dried onion flakes

¼ teaspoon dried basil

¼ teaspoon dried parsley

¼ teaspoon dried oregano

6 chicken drumsticks

1. In a heavy-duty, gallon-sized, zip-top bag mix together the seasoning ingredients: crushed tortilla chips, olive oil, salt, paprika, celery seeds, pepper, garlic powder, onion flakes, basil, parsley, and oregano.

2. To prepare the slow cooker either wrap 4–5 small potatoes in foil and place them in the bottom of a greased 4-quart slow cooker, or make 4–5 foil balls about the size of a small potato and place them in the bottom of the slow cooker. (This will help the chicken to get a little bit crispy in the slow cooker instead of cooking in its juices.)

3. Place 2 drumsticks in the bag with the seasoning mix, seal it tightly, and shake the bag to coat the chicken. Place coated chicken drumsticks on top of the foil balls. Repeat with remaining drumsticks, 2 at a time.

4. Cover the slow cooker and vent the lid with a chopstick to help release extra moisture. Cook on high for 4 hours or on low for 8 hours.

Slow Cooker Suggestions

Double or triple the batch of the seasoned coating ingredients so in the future you can prepare this delicious gluten-free appetizer or light meal in a snap.

Honey-Glazed Chicken Drumsticks

SERVES

4

2 pounds chicken drumsticks

1 tablespoon melted butter

¼ cup lemon juice

¾ cup honey

1 teaspoon sesame oil

3 cloves garlic, peeled and crushed

½ teaspoon ground ginger

½ teaspoon salt

1. Place chicken drumsticks in a greased 4-quart slow cooker.
2. In a glass measuring cup whisk together the melted butter, lemon juice, honey, sesame oil, garlic, ginger, and salt.
3. Pour the honey sauce over the drumsticks. Cook on high for 3–4 hours or on low for 6–8 hours.

Slow Cooker Suggestions

Sesame oil is a highly flavored oil made from pressing either toasted or plain sesame seeds. It provides a unique nutty and earthy flavor to savory dishes. A little goes a long way and it's not very expensive. It can be found at most grocery stores in the Asian aisle.

Chicken Drumsticks with Gluten-Free Stuffing

4

1 onion, peeled and chopped

½ cup chopped celery

2 tablespoons butter

2 teaspoons poultry seasoning

4 cups gluten-free bread, toasted and cubed

½ cup Chicken Broth (see recipe in Chapter 2)

¼ cup dried cranberries

2 large (about 3 pounds) chicken drumsticks

2 slices bacon

½ teaspoon salt

½ teaspoon ground black pepper

1. In a large glass bowl place onion, celery, butter, and poultry seasoning. Cook in the microwave on high for 2 minutes until the vegetables have softened.
2. Add bread cubes and broth to the softened vegetables. Stir in the dried cranberries. Pour stuffing into the bottom of a greased 4-quart slow cooker.
3. Place chicken drumsticks on top of stuffing. Place a piece of bacon on each drumstick. Sprinkle salt and pepper evenly over chicken.
4. Cook on high for 3 hours or on low for 6 hours. Each chicken drumstick makes 2 servings.
5. Cut chicken off of the bone and serve over stuffing.

50 Slow Cooker Favorites: Chicken

CHAPTER 5

Soups

52 Chicken Noodle Soup

53 Comforting Chicken and Rice Soup

54 Tortilla Soup

55 Chicken Vegetable Soup

55 Greek-Style Orzo and Spinach Soup

56 Murghi ka Shorba (Chicken Soup)

57 Greek Lemon-Chicken Soup

58 Aromatic Chicken Rice Soup

58 Simple Ground Chicken and Vegetable Soup

59 Tlalpeño Soup

59 Chicken Congee

60 Vietnamese Cucumber Soup

61 Chicken Mulligatawny Soup

62 Chicken Soup with Lukshen (Noodles)

63 Chicken and Wild Rice Soup

64 Herbed Chicken and Vegetable Soup

Chicken Noodle Soup

4 bone-in chicken thighs, skin removed

2 bone-in chicken breasts, skin removed

4 large carrots, peeled and sliced

1 large sweet onion, peeled and diced

2 celery stalks, diced

1 teaspoon salt

2 teaspoons dried parsley

¾ teaspoon dried marjoram

½ teaspoon dried basil

¼ teaspoon poultry seasoning

¼ teaspoon freshly ground black pepper

1 bay leaf

8 cups water, divided

2½ cups medium egg noodles, uncooked

2 large eggs

1. Add the chicken thighs and breasts, carrots, onion, celery, salt, parsley, marjoram, basil, poultry seasoning, black pepper, bay leaf, and 6 cups of the water to the slow cooker. Cover and cook on low for 8 hours. Move the chicken to a cutting board. Remove and discard the bay leaf.

2. Increase the temperature of the slow cooker to high. Add the remaining 2 cups of water. Stir in the noodles and cook, covered, on high for 20 minutes or until the noodles are cooked through.

3. While the noodles cook, remove the meat from the bones. Cut the chicken into bite-sized pieces or shred it with 2 forks.

4. Ladle about ½ cup of the broth from the slow cooker into a bowl. Add the eggs and whisk to mix; stir the egg mixture into the slow cooker along with the chicken. Cover and cook for 15 minutes.

Comforting Chicken and Rice Soup

SERVES 8

1 tablespoon extra-virgin olive oil

1 medium onion, peeled and chopped

2 cloves garlic, peeled and minced

2 celery stalks, halved lengthwise, and cut into ½"-thick slices

2 medium carrots, peeled and cut diagonally into ½"-thick slices

4 fresh thyme sprigs

1 bay leaf

2 quarts (8 cups) Chicken Broth (see recipe in Chapter 2)

1 cup water

1 cup uncooked long-grain white rice

4 large boneless, skinless chicken breasts

1 teaspoon salt

1 teaspoon ground black pepper

1. In a large skillet heat the olive oil. Add the onion, garlic, and celery. Cook and stir for about 6 minutes, until the vegetables are softened but not browned.

2. Add softened vegetables to a greased 6-quart slow cooker. Add remaining ingredients to the slow cooker.

3. Cover and cook on high for 4–6 hours or on low for 8–10 hours.

4. One hour prior to serving, use 2 forks to shred cooked chicken in the slow cooker and stir throughout the soup.

Tortilla Soup

1 teaspoon cumin powder

1 teaspoon chili powder

1 teaspoon smoked paprika

⅛ teaspoon salt

28 ounces canned crushed tomatoes

1 (14-ounce) can fire-roasted diced tomatoes

3 cups Chicken Broth (see recipe in Chapter 2)

2 cloves garlic, peeled and minced

1 medium onion, peeled and diced

1 (4-ounce) can diced green chilies, drained

2 habanero peppers, seeded and diced

1 cup fresh corn kernels

2 cups cubed cooked boneless chicken breast

4 corn tortillas (see sidebar)

1. Place cumin, chili powder, paprika, salt, tomatoes, broth, garlic, onion, chilies, and peppers in a 4-quart slow cooker. Cover and cook on low for 6 hours.

2. Add the corn and cooked chicken. Cover and cook for an additional 45–60 minutes.

Slow Cooker Suggestions

Slice 4 corn tortillas in half, then into ¼" strips. Heat ½ teaspoon canola oil in a shallow skillet. Add the tortilla strips and cook, turning once, until they are crisp and golden. Drain on paper towel–lined plates. Blot dry. Divide evenly among the bowls of soup before serving.

Chicken Vegetable Soup

SERVES 4

½ cup chopped onions

1 (14.5-ounce) can Italian-seasoned diced tomatoes

1 (15-ounce) can low-sodium Veg-All mixed vegetables

14.5 ounces Chicken Broth (1 can equivalent; see recipe in Chapter 2)

1 (10-ounce) can chunk chicken

1. Place onions in a small glass (or microwave-safe) bowl. Cover with plastic wrap and cook on high for 1–2 minutes until onions are soft.

2. Add softened onions, tomatoes, mixed vegetables, and Chicken Broth to a 2.5-quart or larger slow cooker. Cook on high for 4 hours or on low for 8 hours.

3. Thirty minutes prior to serving add the chicken to the slow cooker. Stir to warm through.

Greek-Style Orzo and Spinach Soup

SERVES 6

2 cloves garlic, peeled and minced

3 tablespoons lemon juice

1 teaspoon lemon zest

5 cups Chicken Stock (see recipe in Chapter 2)

1 small onion, peeled and thinly sliced

1 cup cubed cooked chicken breast

⅓ cup dried orzo

4 cups fresh baby spinach leaves

1. Add the garlic, lemon juice, zest, stock, and onions to a 4-quart slow cooker. Cover and cook on low for 6–8 hours.

2. Stir in the chicken and cook for 30 minutes on high. Add the orzo and spinach. Stir and continue to cook on high for an additional 15 minutes. Stir before serving.

Murghi ka Shorba (Chicken Soup)

1 tablespoon butter

1½ teaspoons cumin seeds

1 teaspoon turmeric powder

2 pounds boneless, skinless chicken breast, cut into large chunks

1 (8-ounce) can diced tomatoes, drained

5 cups Chicken Stock (see recipe in Chapter 2)

1½ teaspoons garam masala

1 teaspoon ground cayenne powder

¼ teaspoon salt

1 cup thick hung yogurt

1. Add the butter to a 6-quart slow cooker. Add the cumin seeds and turmeric. Turn the slow cooker to high setting. Cover. As soon as the butter melts, add the rest of the ingredients except for the yogurt. Cover again and cook for 4 hours on high, or for 7–8 hours on low, or until the chicken is well cooked. Stir occasionally.
2. Serve hot with a dollop of yogurt.

Slow Cooker Suggestions

Do not forget to brown the chicken on the stovetop for 5 minutes before dropping it in the slow cooker.

Greek Lemon-Chicken Soup

4 cups Chicken Broth (see recipe in Chapter 2)

¼ cup fresh lemon juice

¼ cup shredded carrots

¼ cup chopped onion

¼ cup chopped celery

⅛ teaspoon ground white pepper

2 tablespoons butter

2 tablespoons brown rice flour

4 egg yolks

½ cup cooked white rice

½ cup diced, cooked boneless chicken breast

8 slices lemon

1. In a greased 4-quart slow cooker combine the Chicken Broth, lemon juice, carrots, onion, celery, and pepper. Cover and cook on high for 3–4 hours or on low for 6–8 hours.

2. One hour before serving, blend the butter and the flour together in a medium bowl with a fork. Remove 1 cup of hot broth from the slow cooker and whisk with the butter and flour. Add mixture back to the slow cooker.

3. In a small bowl, beat the egg yolks until light in color. Gradually add some of the hot soup to the egg yolks, stirring constantly. Return the egg mixture to the slow cooker.

4. Add the rice and cooked chicken. Cook on low for an additional hour. Ladle hot soup into bowls and garnish with lemon slices.

Aromatic Chicken Rice Soup

2 quarts Chicken Stock (see recipe in Chapter 2)

2 carrots, peeled and diced

2 celery stalks, diced

2" knob fresh ginger, peeled and minced

½" knob galangal root, peeled and minced

2 tablespoons lime juice

1 onion, peeled and minced

4 cloves garlic, peeled and minced

⅛ teaspoon salt

½ teaspoon freshly ground black pepper

½ cup minced fresh cilantro leaves

1½ cups cooked rice

2 cups diced cooked chicken

1. Place the Chicken Stock, carrots, celery, ginger, galangal root, lime juice, onion, garlic, salt, and pepper in a 4-quart slow cooker. Stir. Cook on low for 7–9 hours.

2. Stir in the cilantro, rice, and chicken. Cook on high for 15–30 minutes. Stir prior to serving.

Simple Ground Chicken and Vegetable Soup

1 tablespoon olive oil

1 pound ground chicken

1 medium onion, peeled and diced

2 cloves garlic, peeled and minced

1 (16-ounce) package frozen mixed vegetables

4 cups Chicken Broth (see recipe in Chapter 2)

½ teaspoon ground black pepper

1. In a large skillet over medium heat, add olive oil and heat until sizzling. Cook ground chicken until browned, about 5–6 minutes, stirring to break up the meat. Add meat to a greased 4-quart slow cooker.

2. In the same skillet, sauté onion and garlic until softened, about 3–5 minutes. Add to the slow cooker.

3. Add remaining ingredients. Cover and cook on high for 4 hours or on low for 8 hours.

Tlalpeño Soup

1 teaspoon canola oil

1 small onion, peeled and diced

2 carrots, peeled and diced

2 celery stalks, diced

1 (4-ounce) can diced green chilies, drained

2 chipotle chilies in adobo, minced

1 (15-ounce) can chickpeas, drained

1 tablespoon adobo, from the can of chipotle chilies in adobo

6 cups Chicken Stock (see recipe in Chapter 2)

3 cups diced cooked chicken

1. Heat the oil in a nonstick skillet. Sauté the onions, carrots, and celery until the onions are translucent and the carrots are slightly softened.

2. Place the sautéed vegetables, both kinds of chilies, chickpeas, adobo, and stock into a 4-quart slow cooker. Stir. Cook on low up to 9 hours.

3. About 30–40 minutes before serving, stir in the chicken, and cook on high.

Chicken Congee

4 cups Chicken Stock (see recipe in Chapter 2)

1 cup water

½ cup uncooked long-grain rice

1 teaspoon ground ginger

1 cooked chicken breast, shredded

2 teaspoons soy sauce

3 green onions, green parts thinly sliced

1. Combine Chicken Stock, water, rice, and ground ginger in a 4-quart slow cooker. Cover and cook on high for 2–3 hours or until rice breaks up and soup thickens.

2. Uncover and add chicken. Re-cover and continue to heat for another 30 minutes.

3. Uncover and stir in soy sauce.

4. Ladle soup into bowls. Garnish with green onions. Serve hot.

Vietnamese Cucumber Soup

2 quarts water

1 pound ground chicken

6 tablespoons fish sauce, divided

⅛ teaspoon ground black pepper

4 large cucumbers, peeled, halved, de-seeded, and sliced

2 green onions, chopped

1. Get the water simmering in a large pot (to be placed inside a 6-quart slow cooker).
2. In a large bowl, combine the meat with 2 tablespoons of the fish sauce. Add the pepper, and mix thoroughly.
3. Make meatballs out of the meat mixture and then transfer into boiling water, along with the cucumber slices. Cook for 15 minutes, and be sure to remove any foam and discard. Transfer the whole boiling pot into the slow cooker.
4. Add the green onions and 4 remaining tablespoons of fish sauce. Cover and cook on high for 1½–2 hours.

Chicken Mulligatawny Soup

1 pound boneless, skinless
  chicken breast

3 tablespoons butter

2 apples

2 onions, peeled

¼ cup flour

1½ tablespoons
  curry powder

6 cups Chicken Broth (see
  recipe in Chapter 2)

1 cup uncooked rice

½ teaspoon salt

1. Cube the chicken. Sauté in butter in a pan over medium heat until lightly browned.
2. Core and cube the apples and mince the onions. Add the apples and onions to the chicken in the pan over medium heat and stir until the onions are soft. Add the flour and curry powder and stir to blend in.
3. Put the sautéed mixture, broth, rice, and salt in the slow cooker.
4. Cover and heat on a low setting for 4–6 hours.

Slow Cooker Suggestions

When serving curry, include a variety of garnishes from which guests can choose. Set out chutney, chopped peanuts or cashews, raisins stewed in brandy, sliced hard-boiled eggs, and grated coconut. Also provide thin banana and apple slices doused with lemon juice to prevent browning.

Chicken Soup with Lukshen (Noodles)

1 small potato, peeled and diced

1 parsnip, peeled and cut into chunks

2 carrots, peeled, cut lengthwise then thinly sliced

1 small turnip, peeled and diced

1 celery stalk, diced

2 medium onions, peeled and cut into chunks

1 whole chicken (3½ pounds), cut into quarters or eighths, most of skin removed

1 tablespoon fresh thyme leaves

2 teaspoons minced fresh rosemary leaves

½ teaspoon whole black peppercorns

1 bay leaf

4 sprigs fresh dill

2 sprigs fresh parsley

1 teaspoon kosher salt

8 cups water

1 (12-ounce) bag fine egg noodles

1. Place all ingredients except noodles into a 6-quart slow cooker in order listed. Cover and cook on low for 8–10 hours.

2. Use a slotted spoon to remove and discard parsley, dill, peppercorns, and bay leaf. Transfer chicken to a cutting board, and let cool enough to handle safely.

3. Meanwhile, add noodles to the slow cooker, cover, and continue to cook for another 15–20 minutes or until noodles are tender.

4. Discard skin of cooled chicken. Remove meat from the chicken bones and dice it; add 2 cups back to pot; freeze remaining diced chicken for future use. Discard bones.

5. Ladle soup into bowls and serve hot.

Slow Cooker Suggestions

Take a 7" or 8" square of cheesecloth and place peppercorns, bay leaf, dill, and parsley in the center. Put the corners together, twist, and tie with food-safe twine. Add your just-made packet, called a bouquet garni, to the soup before cooking. At the end of the cooking time simply pull out the bouquet garni and discard.

Chicken and Wild Rice Soup

SERVES
6

6 cups Chicken Broth (see recipe in Chapter 2)

1 cup water

½ cup finely chopped green onions

½ cup uncooked wild rice

⅓ cup butter

¼ cup brown rice flour

½ teaspoon salt

¼ teaspoon poultry seasoning

⅛ teaspoon ground black pepper

2 cups half-and-half

8 slices bacon, cooked and crumbled

1½ cups diced cooked chicken breast

2 tablespoons dry sherry

1. In a greased 4- to 6-quart slow cooker combine Chicken Broth, water, green onions, and wild rice. Cover and cook on high for 4 hours or on low for 8 hours.

2. One hour prior to serving, melt the butter in a medium saucepan over medium-low heat. Whisk in flour, salt, poultry seasoning, and pepper all at once. Cook, stirring, until smooth and bubbly.

3. Stir the half-and-half into the saucepan and cook until thickened, about 2 minutes.

4. Add thickened cream to soup. Then stir in the bacon, chicken, and sherry. Cook on low for an additional hour and serve.

Slow Cooker Suggestions

You can buy precooked and crumbled bacon next to the salad dressings in the grocery store or you can make your own. Cooked and crumbled bacon will keep for several months in the freezer in a sealed zip-top bag.

Herbed Chicken and Vegetable Soup

SERVES
8

7 large carrots

2 celery stalks, finely diced

1 large sweet onion, peeled and diced

8 ounces fresh mushrooms, cleaned and sliced

1 tablespoon extra-virgin olive oil

1 teaspoon butter, melted

1 clove garlic, peeled and minced

4 cups Chicken Broth (see recipe in Chapter 2)

6 medium potatoes, peeled and diced

1 tablespoon dried parsley

¼ teaspoon dried oregano

¼ teaspoon dried rosemary

1 bay leaf

2 strips orange zest

¼ teaspoon salt

¼ teaspoon freshly ground black pepper

8 chicken thighs, skin removed

1 (10-ounce) package frozen green beans, thawed

1 (10-ounce) package frozen whole kernel corn, thawed

1 (10-ounce) package frozen baby peas, thawed

1. Peel the carrots. Dice 6 of the carrots and grate 1. Add the grated carrot, celery, onion, mushrooms, oil, and butter to the slow cooker. Stir to coat the vegetables in the oil and butter. Cover and cook on high for 30 minutes or until the vegetables are soft.

2. Stir in the garlic. Add the broth, diced carrots, potatoes, dried parsley, oregano, rosemary, bay leaf, orange zest, salt, pepper, and chicken thighs. Cover and cook on low for 6 hours.

3. Use a slotted spoon to remove the thighs, cut the meat from the bone and into bite-sized pieces, and return it to the pot. Remove and discard the orange zest and bay leaf. Stir in the green beans, corn, and peas; cover and cook on low for 1 hour or until the vegetables are heated through.

CHAPTER 6

Chili and Stews

66 Fiery Chicken Chili

67 Lean Green Chili

68 Spicy Sausage Chili

68 California Chili

69 Summer Chili

70 Chicken Chili Verde

71 Chicken and Sweet Potato Stew

71 Chicken Corn Chowder

72 Eastern North Carolina Brunswick Stew

73 Creamy Chicken Stew

74 Chicken and Mushroom Stew

74 Tuscan Chicken and Sausage Stew

75 Rosemary-Thyme Stew

76 Easy Chicken and Rice Chili

77 Chicken-Tomatillo Chili

78 Chicken Stew with Meat Sauce

Fiery Chicken Chili

1 pound ground chicken

3 cloves garlic, peeled and chopped

3 chipotle chilies in adobo

1 (15-ounce) can dark red kidney beans, drained and rinsed

1 (15-ounce) can black beans, drained and rinsed

1 teaspoon Worcestershire sauce

2 (14.5-ounce) cans diced tomatoes

1 (4-ounce) can diced green chilies

1 teaspoon ground cayenne powder

1 teaspoon ground chipotle powder

1 onion, peeled and chopped

1 tablespoon habanero hot sauce

1 teaspoon paprika

1 teaspoon hot chili powder

1 teaspoon liquid smoke

1. Quickly sauté the ground chicken in a nonstick skillet until just cooked through. Drain all fat.
2. Place all ingredients in a 4-quart slow cooker. Stir. Cook on low for 8–10 hours.

Slow Cooker Suggestions

Liquid smoke is made by condensing smoke in water to form a fluid. It is found in a variety of flavors including hickory and mesquite and can be used to add the flavor of being slow-cooked over a flame without actually having to grill.

Lean Green Chili

2 (15-ounce) cans cannellini beans, drained and rinsed

1 teaspoon cumin powder

1 teaspoon ground jalapeño powder

1 jalapeño pepper, minced

2 cloves garlic, peeled and minced

1 (4-ounce) can diced green chilies, drained

1 (28-ounce) can tomatillos, drained

1 medium onion, peeled and diced

1 tablespoon lime juice

1 teaspoon celery flakes

1 celery stalk, diced

2 cups diced cooked chicken breast

Place all of the ingredients except the chicken in a 4-quart slow cooker. Cook on low for 8 hours. Stir in the chicken, put the lid back on, and cook for an additional hour on low. Stir before serving.

Slow Cooker Suggestions

Cube leftover cooked chicken breast and freeze in clearly marked 1- or 2-cup packages. Defrost overnight in the refrigerator before using. Cooked poultry should be added to a recipe during the last hour of cooking.

Spicy Sausage Chili

1½ pounds spicy chicken sausage

2 teaspoons ground cayenne powder

1 tablespoon ground chipotle powder

1 teaspoon hot paprika

1 teaspoon hot chili powder

1 (15-ounce) can cannellini beans, drained and rinsed

1 (14.5-ounce) can tomatoes with green chilies

1 (15-ounce) can hominy

1 teaspoon cumin powder

1. Brown the sausage in a nonstick skillet. Drain off all fat.

2. Add the sausage and remaining ingredients to a 4-quart slow cooker and stir to combine. Break up the hominy as needed. Cook on low for 8–10 hours.

California Chili

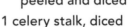

1 (15-ounce) can hominy

1 (14.5-ounce) can fire-roasted tomatoes with garlic

½ cup canned cannellini beans, drained and rinsed

1 teaspoon cumin powder

1 teaspoon ground jalapeño powder

2 Anaheim chilies, diced

6 cloves garlic, peeled and thinly sliced

1 medium onion, peeled and diced

1 celery stalk, diced

1 tablespoon lime juice

1 teaspoon ground chipotle powder

1 teaspoon ground California chili powder

2 cups diced cooked chicken breast

1. Place all of the ingredients except the chicken in a 4-quart slow cooker. Cook on low for 8 hours.

2. Stir in the chicken, cover the cooker again, and cook for an additional hour on low. Stir before serving.

Summer Chili

½ pound ground chicken

1 bulb fennel, diced

4 radishes, diced

2 celery stalks, diced, including leaves

2 carrots, peeled and cut into coin-sized pieces

1 medium onion, peeled and diced

1 shallot, peeled and diced

4 cloves garlic, peeled and sliced

1 habanero pepper, diced

1 (15-ounce) can cannellini beans, drained and rinsed

2 (6-ounce) cans tomato paste

½ teaspoon dried oregano

½ teaspoon ground black pepper

½ teaspoon crushed dried rosemary

½ teaspoon ground cayenne powder

½ teaspoon ground chipotle powder

1 teaspoon chili powder

1 teaspoon tarragon

¼ teaspoon cumin powder

¼ teaspoon celery seed

2 zucchini, cubed

10 Campari tomatoes, quartered

1 cup corn kernels

1. Sauté the ground chicken in a nonstick pan until just browned. Add to a 4-quart slow cooker along with the fennel, radishes, celery, carrots, onion, shallot, garlic, habanero, beans, tomato paste, and all spices. Stir.

2. Cook on low for 6–7 hours; then stir in the zucchini, tomatoes, and corn. Cook for an additional 30 minutes on high. Stir before serving.

Chicken Chili Verde

½ tablespoon olive oil

2 pounds skinless, boneless chicken breast, cubed

2 (28-ounce) cans whole peeled tomatoes, undrained

1 (16-ounce) can chili beans, drained and rinsed

1 (15-ounce) can kidney beans, drained and rinsed

1 (4-ounce) can diced green chilies, undrained

1 tablespoon Italian seasoning

1 tablespoon chili powder

2 teaspoons cumin powder

1 tablespoon sugar

1 onion, peeled and minced

3 cloves garlic, peeled and minced

½ cup water

1. Heat oil in a skillet over medium heat. Add the chicken. Cook, stirring frequently, until chicken is browned on all sides, about 1–2 minutes per side. Place browned chicken in a greased 4- to 6-quart slow cooker.

2. Add remaining ingredients over the chicken in the slow cooker.

3. Cover and cook on high for 3 hours or on low for 6 hours.

Slow Cooker Suggestions

If you have a second slow cooker, you can use it to make rice while the chili is cooking. To make rice: grease a 2.5-quart or larger slow cooker with butter or nonstick spray. Add 1 cup of raw white rice, ½ teaspoon salt, and 2 cups of water. Cover and cook on high for 1½–2½ hours until rice is cooked through, has absorbed liquids, and is fluffy.

Chicken and Sweet Potato Stew

1 pound boneless, skinless chicken breast, cubed

12 ounces sweet potatoes, peeled and cubed

12 ounces Chicken Stock (see recipe in Chapter 2)

1 large green bell pepper, sliced

3 teaspoons chili powder

½ teaspoon garlic powder

¼ cup cold water

2 tablespoons almond meal

¼ teaspoon ground black pepper

1. Combine all ingredients except water, almond meal, and black pepper in a 4-quart slow cooker. Cover and cook on high 4–5 hours.

2. In a small bowl, combine the almond meal and water. Add to the slow cooker, stirring 2–3 minutes. Season with black pepper.

Chicken Corn Chowder

1 pound boneless chicken breast, cut into ½" pieces

2 (14.5-ounce) cans Mexican-style diced tomatoes

1 (10-ounce) can sweet whole kernel corn, drained

1 (8-ounce) package cream cheese

1. Add chicken breast, diced tomatoes, and sweet corn to a greased 4-quart slow cooker. Cook on high for 4 hours or on low for 8 hours.

2. Twenty minutes prior to serving stir in cream cheese. If desired, serve with gluten-free corn chips and guacamole.

Eastern North Carolina Brunswick Stew

¼ cup unsalted butter

1 large yellow onion, peeled and diced

2 quarts (8 cups) water

1 pound boneless, skinless chicken breast

1 pound boneless, skinless chicken thighs

2 cups pulled pork, chopped

1 (15-ounce) can green beans, undrained

2 (8-ounce) cans baby lima beans, undrained

2 (28-ounce) cans whole tomatoes, undrained and chopped

3 medium potatoes, peeled and diced

1 (15-ounce) can sweet corn

⅓ cup sugar

2 teaspoons hot sauce

2 teaspoons salt

1 teaspoon ground black pepper

1. In a skillet heat butter until sizzling and cook onion until softened and fragrant, about 3–5 minutes. Add onion to a 6-quart slow cooker.

2. Add remaining ingredients, except salt and pepper. Cook on high for 4 hours or on low for 8 hours.

3. One hour before serving, remove chicken and shred using 2 forks. Return chicken to the soup. Add salt and pepper.

Slow Cooker Suggestions

The origins of Brunswick Stew have been debated for years. Some say the stew originated in Georgia; others say it began in Virginia. The stew is usually tomato-based with lima beans, corn, okra, and other vegetables. The meats used can vary. Many old recipes call for wild meats such as rabbit and squirrel. In eastern North Carolina it's often served in restaurants with shredded pork barbecue, vinegary coleslaw, and corn bread.

Creamy Chicken Stew

2 tablespoons olive oil

3 pounds boneless, skinless chicken breast, cut into 1" cubes

1 teaspoon salt

1 teaspoon ground black pepper

1 teaspoon paprika

2 cups white potatoes, peeled and cubed

3 large carrots, peeled and diced

2 cups frozen whole kernel corn

1 cup chopped green bell pepper

1 cup chopped sweet red bell pepper

1 cup diced celery

1 medium onion, peeled and diced

2 teaspoons dried basil

1 bay leaf

¼ teaspoon celery salt

7 cups Chicken Broth (see recipe in Chapter 2)

½ cup butter

⅓ cup brown rice flour

1. In a large skillet, heat olive oil. Sauté chicken pieces in small batches until they are browned, about 1–2 minutes per side. Add browned chicken to a greased 6-quart slow cooker.

2. Add salt, pepper, paprika, potatoes, carrots, corn, green and red peppers, celery, onion, basil, bay leaf, celery salt, and Chicken Broth to the slow cooker. Cover and cook on high for 4 hours or on low for 8 hours. One hour before serving remove bay leaf.

3. In a large saucepan, melt butter; whisk in flour until smooth. Cook and stir for 2 minutes. Gradually whisk in 2 cups of hot broth from the slow cooker. Bring to a boil; cook and stir for 2 minutes or until thickened. Whisk thickened sauce into stew in the slow cooker. Cook an additional hour.

Chicken and Mushroom Stew

SERVES 6

1 pound boneless chicken, cut into 1" cubes, browned (in olive oil)

1 tablespoon olive oil

8 ounces fresh mushrooms, cleaned and sliced

1 medium onion, peeled and diced

3 cups diced zucchini

1 cup diced green bell pepper

4 garlic cloves, peeled and minced

3 medium tomatoes, diced

1 (6-ounce) can tomato paste

¾ cup water

1 teaspoon each: dried thyme, oregano, marjoram, and basil

1. Add browned chicken to a 4- to 6-quart slow cooker.

2. Add olive oil to a sauté pan and over medium heat, sauté the mushrooms, onion, zucchini, green pepper, and garlic for 5–10 minutes, until crisp-tender, and add to the slow cooker.

3. Add the tomatoes, tomato paste, water, and seasonings.

4. Cover and cook on low for 4 hours or until the vegetables are tender. Serve hot.

Tuscan Chicken and Sausage Stew

SERVES 4

1 pound boneless, skinless chicken thighs

8 ounces chicken sausage, cut into ½" slices

1 (26-ounce) jar gluten-free pasta sauce

1 (14.5-ounce) can green beans, drained

1 teaspoon dried oregano

1. Cut chicken thighs into bite-sized pieces. Place chicken into a greased 4-quart slow cooker.

2. Add remaining ingredients. Stir to combine and cook on high for 4 hours or on low for 8 hours.

Rosemary-Thyme Stew

1 teaspoon canola oil

1 large onion, peeled and diced

1 tablespoon flour

1 carrot, peeled and diced

2 celery stalks, diced

2 cloves garlic, peeled and minced

1 cup diced Yukon Gold potatoes

3½ tablespoons minced fresh thyme leaves

3 tablespoons minced fresh rosemary leaves

1 pound boneless skinless chicken breast, cut into 1" cubes

¼ teaspoon salt

½ teaspoon freshly ground black pepper

1½ cups Chicken Stock (see recipe in Chapter 2)

½ cup frozen corn kernels

1. Heat the oil in a large skillet. Sauté the onion, flour, carrots, celery, garlic, potatoes, thyme, rosemary, and chicken until the chicken is white on all sides. Drain off any excess fat.

2. Put sautéed ingredients into a 4-quart slow cooker. Sprinkle with salt and pepper. Pour in the stock. Stir. Cook for 8–9 hours on low.

3. Add the corn. Cover and cook an additional ½ hour on high. Stir before serving.

Easy Chicken and Rice Chili

1 pound ground chicken

¼ cup chopped onion

1 (14.5-ounce) can diced tomatoes

3 teaspoons chili powder

1 teaspoon cumin powder

1 teaspoon garlic powder

2 (15-ounce) cans kidney beans, undrained

1½ cups water

1 cup cooked white rice

1. Brown ground chicken in a large skillet for about 5–6 minutes, until cooked through. Add onion and cook for 2–3 minutes until softened.
2. Place browned ground chicken and onions in a greased 4-quart slow cooker. Add tomatoes, chili powder, cumin, garlic powder, kidney beans, and water. Stir to combine. Cover and cook on high for 2–3 hours or on low for 5–6 hours.
3. An hour before serving stir in cooked rice.

Chicken-Tomatillo Chili

SERVES
8

2 cups cubed tomatillos

1 green bell pepper, diced

1 onion, peeled and diced

1 teaspoon ground cayenne powder

1 teaspoon cumin powder

1 teaspoon paprika

1 teaspoon chili powder

1 (30-ounce) can chili beans, drained and rinsed

2 cups cubed cooked chicken breast

Place all ingredients except the chicken in a 4-quart slow cooker. Stir to mix the ingredients. Cook on low for 8 hours, and then stir in the chicken. Cook for an additional 30–60 minutes on high.

Slow Cooker Suggestions

Tomatillos, like tomatoes, are a part of the nightshade family of vegetables. They look like small tomatoes covered in a papery husk. The husk should be removed before eating. Look for tomatillos that are unblemished, slightly heavy for their size, and solid to the touch. They are most commonly green but can also be purple or yellow.

Chicken Stew with Meat Sauce

SERVES
4

1 pound (90% lean) grass-fed ground beef

4 boneless, skinless chicken breasts

1 (6-ounce) can organic tomato paste

1 (28-ounce) can diced organic tomatoes, no salt added

4 garlic cloves, peeled and chopped

4 large carrots, peeled and sliced

2 red bell peppers, diced

2 green bell peppers, diced

1 tablespoon dried thyme

2 tablespoons olive oil

1 tablespoon chili powder

1. In a medium sauté pan, cook ground beef until browned, about 5 minutes. Drain and place in a 4- to 6-quart slow cooker.
2. Wipe out the sauté pan and place it over medium-high heat. Brown the chicken breasts 5 minutes per side. Add to the slow cooker.
3. Combine all the remaining ingredients in the slow cooker. Cook on high for 5 hours.
4. Serve over your favorite steamed vegetable.

Slow Cooker Suggestions

Slow cookers are the greatest appliance for the Paleo enthusiast. These little countertop cookers allow you to cook easily and in bulk, which is important for a successful Paleolithic dieter.

CHAPTER 7

Comforting Favorites

80 Chicken and Dumplings

81 No-Crust Chicken Potpie

81 Cinnamon Chicken Pasta

82 Biscuit-Topped Chicken Pie

83 Chicken and Gravy

83 Easy Chicken and Dressing

84 Scalloped Chicken

84 Chicken Stroganoff

85 Chicken Cacciatore

86 Chicken in Lemon Sauce

87 Chicken, Broccoli, and Rice Casserole

88 Chicken Paprikash

89 Creamy Chicken in a Mushroom and White Wine Sauce

90 Barbecue Chicken

90 Honey-Mustard Chicken

Chicken and Dumplings

1 tablespoon canola oil

1 onion, peeled and chopped

3 cloves garlic, peeled and minced

1 cup diced cremini mushrooms

2 carrots, peeled and diced

2 celery stalks, diced

1 parsnip, peeled and diced

1 jalapeño pepper, seeded and diced

½ teaspoon salt

½ teaspoon ground black pepper

1 large red skin potato, diced

½ teaspoon dried dill weed

½ teaspoon ground cayenne powder

6 cups Chicken Stock (see recipe in Chapter 2)

3 cups diced, cooked chicken breast

1 tablespoon baking powder

2 cups flour

¾ cup fat-free buttermilk

2 eggs

¼ cup chopped green onion

1. Heat the canola oil in a small skillet, then add the onions, garlic, and mushrooms. Sauté until softened, about 2 minutes. Add to an oval 4-quart slow cooker along with the carrots, celery, parsnip, jalapeño, salt, pepper, potato, dill weed, cayenne, and stock. Cook on low for 6 hours.

2. Add the cooked chicken and turn up to high.

3. Meanwhile, whisk the baking powder and flour in a medium bowl. Stir in the buttermilk, eggs, and green onion. Mix to combine. Divide the mixture into 3" dumplings.

4. Carefully drop the dumplings one at a time into the slow cooker. Cover and continue to cook on high for 30 minutes or until the dumplings are cooked through and fluffy.

No-Crust Chicken Potpie

Butter-flavored cooking spray

10 ounces coconut milk

1 teaspoon dried parsley

1 teaspoon dried onion flakes

1 (16-ounce) package frozen cauliflower, broccoli, and carrot blend

1 pound skinned and boned uncooked chicken breast, cut into ½" cubes

1. Spray a 4-quart slow cooker with butter-flavored cooking spray.
2. In the prepared slow cooker, combine coconut milk, parsley, and onion flakes.
3. Stir in the frozen vegetables and chicken pieces. Cover and cook on low for 8 hours. Mix well before serving.

Cinnamon Chicken Pasta

3 pounds chicken

½ teaspoon salt

½ teaspoon pepper

½ lemon

½ cup olive oil

6 ounces tomato paste

1 cup water

1 stick cinnamon bark

4 cups cooked pasta, firm

1. Cut the chicken into serving-size pieces. Roll the chicken pieces in salt and pepper, then drizzle with the juice from the ½ lemon. Sauté the chicken pieces in olive oil in a pan over medium heat until lightly browned. Transfer the chicken to a slow cooker, but retain the juices in the pan.
2. Add the tomato paste, water, and cinnamon stick to the same pan and stir over low heat until well mixed with the chicken juices.
3. Pour the tomato mixture over the chicken in the slow cooker.
4. Cover and heat on a low setting for 3–4 hours.
5. Half an hour before serving, stir the pasta into the sauce. Remove cinnamon stick before serving, if not completely dissolved.

Biscuit-Topped Chicken Pie

4 tablespoons brown rice flour

4 tablespoons butter

1 cup whole milk

1 cup Chicken Broth (see recipe in Chapter 2)

1 teaspoon salt

½ teaspoon ground black pepper

2 cups cooked chicken breast, cut into bite-sized pieces

1 (12-ounce) can mixed vegetables, drained

1 (16.3-ounce) package refrigerated buttermilk biscuits

1. In a small saucepan over medium heat, whisk together flour and butter. When the butter has melted, slowly stir in milk, Chicken Broth, salt, and pepper. Cook on medium heat for 5–10 minutes, whisking constantly until mixture is thick, with a gravy consistency.

2. Add chicken and vegetables to a greased 4-quart slow cooker. Pour cream soup mixture into the slow cooker and mix with chicken and vegetables.

3. Separate biscuit dough and place over chicken, vegetables, and sauce.

4. Cover slow cooker and vent lid with a chopstick. Cook on high for 3–4 hours or on low for 6–8 hours until chicken sauce is bubbling up around the biscuits, and the biscuits are cooked through.

Chicken and Gravy

1 (10.75-ounce) can condensed cream of chicken soup

1 (10.5-ounce) can condensed cream of mushroom soup

¼ teaspoon freshly ground black pepper

4 (6-ounce) skinless, boneless chicken breasts

4 medium potatoes, peeled and quartered

Add the soups and pepper to the slow cooker. Stir to combine. Add the chicken breasts, pushing them down into the soup mixture. Add the potatoes in a layer on top. Cover and cook on low for 4–6 hours.

Easy Chicken and Dressing

Nonstick spray

1 (15.75-ounce) can condensed cream of chicken soup

⅓ cup whole milk

4 (8-ounce) boneless, skinless chicken breasts

1 (6-ounce) package chicken-flavored stuffing mix

1⅔ cups water

1. Treat the crock of the slow cooker with nonstick spray. Add the soup and milk; stir to combine. Put the chicken in the slow cooker, pressing it down into the soup.
2. Mix together the stuffing mix and water in a bowl; spoon over the top of the chicken. Cover and cook on low for 8 hours.

Scalloped Chicken

Nonstick spray

1 (5-ounce) box scalloped potatoes

1 (10-ounce) can white meat chicken

3¾ cups water

Treat the slow cooker with nonstick spray. Add the potatoes and sprinkle the seasoning mix over the top of them. Spread the chicken over the top of the potatoes. Pour in the water. Cover and cook on low for 5 hours.

Chicken Stroganoff

SERVES
6

Nonstick spray

1 (10.5-ounce) can condensed cream of mushroom soup

1 (4-ounce) can sliced mushrooms, drained

1 tablespoon Worcestershire sauce

2½ pounds skinless, boneless chicken breast

1 (16-ounce) container sour cream

Cooked, buttered egg noodles

1. Treat crock of the slow cooker with nonstick spray. Add the soup, mushrooms, and Worcestershire sauce; stir to mix.

2. Cut the chicken breast into bite-sized pieces; add to the cooker and stir into the sauce. Cover and cook on low for 8 hours.

3. Stir in the sour cream; cover and continue to cook long enough to bring the sour cream sauce to temperature, or for about 30 minutes. Serve over cooked, buttered egg noodles or, if you prefer, over toast or biscuits.

Chicken Cacciatore

¾ cup brown rice flour, divided

½ teaspoon salt

8 bone-in chicken thighs, skin removed (if using boneless, reduce cooking time by 1 hour)

3 tablespoons olive oil

1 medium yellow onion, peeled and diced

4 cloves garlic, peeled and minced

3 tablespoons coarsely chopped oil-packed sun-dried tomatoes

1 cup dry white wine

⅛ teaspoon dried sage

¼ teaspoon dried rosemary

Pinch dried red pepper flakes

½ teaspoon freshly ground black pepper

1. Add ½ cup of the flour, salt, and the chicken thighs to a gallon-sized plastic bag; close and shake to coat the chicken.

2. Add the oil to a large sauté pan and bring it to medium-high heat. Add the chicken thighs; brown the chicken by cooking the pieces on one side for 5 minutes, and then turning them over and frying them for another 5 minutes. Drain the chicken on paper towels and then place in a 4- to 6-quart slow cooker. Cover the slow cooker and set the temperature to low.

3. Add the onion to the sauté pan and cook until the onions begin to soften, about 3–5 minutes. Stir in the garlic and sauté for 30 seconds. Add the sun-dried tomatoes. Slowly pour the wine into the pan to deglaze (stirring to scrape the browned bits off the bottom of the pan). Stir in the sage, rosemary, pepper flakes, and black pepper and then pour the sauce over the chicken in the slow cooker.

4. Cover and cook on high for 3–4 hours or on low for 6–7 hours.

Chicken in Lemon Sauce

SERVES

4

1 (16-ounce) bag frozen cut green beans, thawed

1 small onion, peeled and cut into thin wedges

4 boneless, skinless chicken breast halves

4 medium potatoes, peeled and cut in quarters

2 cloves garlic, peeled and minced

¼ teaspoon freshly ground black pepper

1 cup Chicken Broth (see recipe in Chapter 2)

4 ounces cream cheese, cut into cubes

1 teaspoon freshly grated lemon peel

Lemon peel strips

1. Place green beans and onion in the slow cooker. Arrange the chicken and potatoes over the vegetables. Sprinkle with the garlic and pepper. Pour broth over all. Cover and cook on low for 5 or more hours or until chicken is cooked through and moist.

2. Evenly divide the chicken, potatoes, and vegetables between 4 serving plates or onto a serving platter; cover to keep warm.

3. To make the sauce, add the cream cheese cubes and grated lemon peel to the broth in the slow cooker. Stir until cheese melts into the sauce. Pour the sauce over the chicken, potatoes, and vegetables. Garnish with lemon peel strips.

Chicken, Broccoli, and Rice Casserole

Nonstick spray

2 (10.75-ounce) cans condensed cream of mushroom soup

1 (15-ounce) jar Cheez Whiz

½ cup mayonnaise

1 tablespoon lemon juice

2 soup cans hot water

½ cup whole milk

2 pounds skinless, boneless chicken breast

1 (8-ounce) can whole water chestnuts, drained

2 (10-ounce) bags frozen broccoli florets, thawed

2 cups instant rice

1 medium onion, peeled and diced

2 celery stalks, diced

1 (4-ounce) can sliced mushrooms, drained

¼ teaspoon salt

¼ teaspoon freshly ground black pepper

¼ teaspoon paprika

1 (4-ounce) bag blanched slivered almonds

1. Treat the slow cooker with nonstick spray. Add the mushroom soup, Cheez Whiz, mayonnaise, lemon juice, water, and milk; stir to combine.

2. Cut the chicken breast into bite-sized pieces and chop the water chestnuts; stir into the soup mixture in the slow cooker along with the broccoli florets, rice, onion, celery, and sliced mushrooms. Cover and cook on high for 4 hours or until the rice is cooked through.

3. Stir in salt and pepper. Sprinkle paprika over the casserole and top with the almonds.

Chicken Paprikash

1 tablespoon butter

1 tablespoon extra-virgin olive oil

1 large yellow onion, peeled and diced

2 cloves garlic, peeled and minced

3 pounds boneless, skinless chicken thighs

½ teaspoon salt

¼ teaspoon freshly ground black pepper

2 tablespoons Hungarian paprika

½ cup Chicken Broth (see recipe in Chapter 2)

¼ cup dry white wine

1 (16-ounce) container sour cream

4 cups cooked gluten-free pasta

1. Add the butter, oil, and onion to a microwave-safe bowl; cover and microwave on high for 1 minute. Stir, re-cover, and microwave on high for another minute or until the onions are transparent. Stir in the garlic; cover and microwave on high for 30 seconds. Add to a greased 4- to 6-quart slow cooker.

2. Cut the chicken thighs into bite-sized pieces. Add the chicken to the slow cooker. Stir in the salt, pepper, paprika, broth, and wine; cover and cook on low for 6 hours or on high for 3 hours.

3. Stir in the sour cream; cover and continue to cook long enough to bring the sour cream sauce to temperature, about 30 minutes. Serve over pasta. Sprinkle each serving with additional paprika if desired. Serve immediately.

Slow Cooker Suggestions

If the resulting sauce for the Chicken Paprikash is too thin, add more sour cream. If it's too thick, slowly whisk in some milk.

Creamy Chicken in a Mushroom and White Wine Sauce

SERVES 4

Nonstick spray

4 boneless chicken breasts, cut into chunks

3 tablespoons cornstarch

1 cup 2% milk

½ cup white wine

½ teaspoon salt

½ teaspoon ground black pepper

1½ teaspoons poultry seasoning

½ teaspoon garlic powder

½ teaspoon salt-free, all-purpose seasoning

2 (4-ounce) cans sliced mushrooms, drained and rinsed

1½ cups frozen peas

2 cups cooked gluten-free pasta

1. Grease a 4-quart slow cooker with nonstick cooking spray. Place chicken into the slow cooker.

2. In a saucepan whisk together the cornstarch, milk, and white wine. Whisk in salt, pepper, poultry seasoning, garlic powder, and salt-free seasoning. Cook over medium heat, whisking constantly until sauce thickens. Pour sauce over chicken.

3. Add mushrooms on top of the chicken. Cook on low for 6 hours or on high for 3 hours.

4. One hour before serving stir in the frozen peas.

5. Serve over pasta.

Barbecue Chicken

½ cup ketchup

2 tablespoons brown sugar

1 tablespoon quick-cooking tapioca

1 tablespoon apple cider vinegar

1 teaspoon Worcestershire sauce

1 teaspoon steak sauce

¼ teaspoon ground cinnamon

⅛ teaspoon ground cloves

¼ teaspoon dried red pepper flakes

2 chicken thighs, skin removed

1. Add the ketchup, brown sugar, tapioca, vinegar, Worcestershire sauce, steak sauce, cinnamon, cloves, and red pepper flakes to the slow cooker; stir to combine.

2. Place the chicken thighs in the slow cooker, meaty side down. Cover and cook on low for 8 or more hours or until the chicken is tender and pulls away from the bone. Remove the chicken; allow to cool enough to remove the meat from the bones. Shred the chicken or cut into pieces. Skim any fat off of the top of the barbecue sauce in the slow cooker. Stir the chicken into the sauce and continue to cook long enough for it to come back to temperature.

Honey-Mustard Chicken

Nonstick spray

2 chicken thighs, skin removed

4 red potatoes, peeled and quartered

¼ cup stone-ground mustard

⅓ cup honey

1 tablespoon apple cider vinegar

1 tablespoon quick-cooking tapioca

Extra-virgin olive oil

Treat the crock of the slow cooker with nonstick spray. Place the thighs in the slow cooker, meaty side down. Layer the potatoes over the thighs. Add the mustard, honey, vinegar, and tapioca to a bowl; mix well, then pour into the slow cooker. Cover and cook on low for 8 hours. When serving, drizzle extra-virgin olive oil over the potatoes.

CHAPTER 8

Classic American Dishes

92 Creole Chicken and Vegetables

93 Hawaiian Chicken

94 Barbecue Chicken and Beans

95 Sweet and Spicy Pulled Chicken

95 Buffalo Chicken Sandwich Filling

96 Ground Chicken Joes

97 Chicken Tenders

97 Saucy Brown Sugar Chicken

98 Molasses Barbecue Chicken

99 Cajun Chicken and Shrimp Creole

100 Chicken Taco Filling

101 Enchilada Filling, Paleo Style

102 Salsa Chicken

102 Chili Beer Chicken

Creole Chicken and Vegetables

SERVES 4

8 boneless, skinless chicken thighs

2 tablespoons Creole seasoning

1 (16-ounce) bag of frozen mixed vegetables such as broccoli, cauliflower, and carrots

1 (15-ounce) can of diced tomatoes

½ teaspoon ground black pepper

1 cup brown rice, uncooked

1. Place chicken thighs in the bottom of a 4-quart greased slow cooker.
2. Sprinkle Creole seasoning over chicken.
3. Add frozen vegetables, tomatoes, and pepper to the slow cooker.
4. Cook on high for 3 hours or on low for 6 hours. An hour before serving stir in the brown rice.

Slow Cooker Suggestions

The Internet has become a valuable research tool to find out if processed foods are gluten-free. Spice mixes can often contain questionable ingredients and it's important to make sure they are safe for your diet. Many company websites have a "frequently asked questions" page that often lists their gluten-free products.

Hawaiian Chicken

SERVES

4

4 boneless, skinless chicken breasts

1 (15-ounce) can sliced pineapple, drained (reserve juice)

½ green bell pepper, sliced

½ red bell pepper, sliced

¼ teaspoon ground cinnamon

½ teaspoon Chinese five-spice powder

½ teaspoon crushed red pepper

1. Place chicken breasts in a greased 4-quart slow cooker.
2. Add 2 slices of pineapple on top of each piece of chicken. If there are leftover pieces, simply set them alongside the chicken.
3. Place red and green pepper slices evenly over all the pieces of chicken. Sprinkle the cinnamon, Chinese five-spice powder, and crushed pepper evenly over the chicken.
4. Finally, pour ½ cup of the reserved pineapple juice over the chicken.
5. Cook on high for 2½–3 hours or on low for 5–6 hours.

Slow Cooker Suggestions

When buying canned fruit try to buy varieties that are canned in natural juices instead of corn syrup. The leftover juice can be saved in the refrigerator to use later as juice to drink, or even as a natural sweetener for a glass of iced tea or a bowl of warm oatmeal.

Barbecue Chicken and Beans

3 (6-ounce) boneless, skinless chicken breasts, cut into 1" pieces

1 (15-ounce) can red kidney beans, drained and rinsed

2 teaspoons gluten-free Worcestershire sauce

1 cup gluten-free homemade (see recipe in sidebar) or store-bought barbecue sauce

2 cups cooked white rice

1. Add all ingredients except rice to a greased 2.5-quart or larger slow cooker.

2. Cook on high for 4 hours or on low for 8 hours. Serve over rice.

Slow Cooker Suggestions

To make your own barbecue sauce, mix together 1 cup gluten-free ketchup, ¼ cup apple cider vinegar, 2 tablespoons brown sugar or molasses, 1 tablespoon Dijon mustard, 1 tablespoon water, ½ teaspoon salt, and ½ teaspoon ground black pepper. Cook over medium heat for 3–5 minutes and let cool. Use as you would any barbecue sauce. Store in an airtight container or a washed, recycled plastic bottle in the refrigerator for up to 1 month.

Sweet and Spicy Pulled Chicken

SERVES 4

1¾ pounds boneless, skinless chicken thighs

¼ cup chili sauce

¼ cup balsamic vinegar

2 tablespoons ginger preserves

2 tablespoons pineapple juice

2 tablespoons lime juice

1 teaspoon ground cayenne powder

½ teaspoon ground chipotle powder

½ teaspoon hot paprika

1 jalapeño pepper, minced

3 cloves garlic, peeled and minced

1 teaspoon yellow hot sauce

1. Place all ingredients in a round 2- or 4-quart slow cooker. Cook on low for 3½ hours, or for 1½ hours on low and then turn it up to high for an additional hour.

2. When done, the meat should shred easily with a fork. Thoroughly shred the chicken then toss to coat it evenly with the sauce.

Buffalo Chicken Sandwich Filling

SERVES 4

4 boneless, skinless chicken thighs

¼ cup diced onion

1 clove garlic, peeled and minced

½ teaspoon freshly ground black pepper

⅛ teaspoon salt

2 cups buffalo wing sauce

1. Place all ingredients in a 4-quart slow cooker. Stir. Cook on high for 2–3 hours or until the chicken is easily shredded with a fork. If the sauce is very thin, cook on high uncovered for 30 minutes or until thickened.

2. Shred the chicken and toss with the sauce.

Ground Chicken Joes

2 teaspoons olive oil

1 pound lean ground chicken

½ cup finely chopped onion

½ cup finely chopped green bell pepper

1 teaspoon garlic powder

1 tablespoon prepared yellow mustard

¾ cup gluten-free ketchup

3 tablespoons brown sugar

1 tablespoon gluten-free Worcestershire sauce

¼ teaspoon salt

½ teaspoon ground black pepper

4 gluten-free hamburger rolls

1. Add olive oil to a large skillet and brown ground chicken, onion, and green pepper for approximately 5–6 minutes. Drain off any grease.

2. Add chicken mixture to a greased 2.5-quart or 4-quart slow cooker. Add garlic powder, mustard, ketchup, brown sugar, Worcestershire sauce, salt, and pepper.

3. Mix ingredients together and cook on low for 4 hours or on high for 2 hours.

4. Serve on hamburger rolls.

Slow Cooker Suggestions

Instead of using this recipe as a sandwich filling you could also serve it over cooked rice, a baked potato, or gluten-free spaghetti noodles for a fun twist. For a Mexican-style variation, leave out the brown sugar and Worcestershire sauce and replace the ketchup with 1 cup of tomato sauce along with 1 packet of gluten-free taco seasoning.

Chicken Tenders

4

2 tablespoons olive oil

1 clove garlic, peeled and minced

6 sprigs of fresh thyme, stripped and chopped

1 tablespoon lemon zest

¼ cup lemon juice

1 pound chicken breast tenders

¼ teaspoon ground black pepper

Nonstick spray

1. In a large mixing bowl, combine the olive oil, garlic, chopped thyme, lemon zest, and lemon juice.

2. Season the chicken tenders with pepper.

3. Spray a 2-quart slow cooker with nonstick cooking spray. Place chicken tenders in the slow cooker, and pour the olive oil mixture over them, stirring until coated.

4. Cover and cook on low for 4–6 hours.

Saucy Brown Sugar Chicken

4

4 skinless, boneless chicken breasts

1 (12-ounce) jar peach salsa

¼ cup brown sugar

1 tablespoon Dijon mustard

1. Place chicken breasts in a greased 4-quart slow cooker.

2. In small bowl mix together salsa, brown sugar, and mustard. Pour over chicken.

3. Cook chicken for 3–4 hours on high or 6–8 hours on low.

Slow Cooker Suggestions

If you have multiple slow cookers you can make several main dishes at one time on Sunday afternoons. The ready-made meals can then be frozen or stored in the refrigerator for up to 5 days. You will save money and time by having homemade slow-cooked meals already prepared.

Molasses Barbecue Chicken

4 boneless, skinless chicken breasts

½ cup ketchup

2 tablespoons apple cider vinegar

2 tablespoons molasses

2 tablespoons brown sugar

1 teaspoon liquid smoke

1½ tablespoons minced dried onions

¼ teaspoon ground cayenne powder

2 teaspoons ground mustard

1. Place chicken in a greased 4-quart slow cooker.
2. In a bowl whisk together the ketchup, vinegar, molasses, brown sugar, liquid smoke, dried onions, cayenne powder, and mustard.
3. Pour the homemade barbecue sauce over the chicken.
4. Cook on low for 6 hours or on high for 3 hours.

Cajun Chicken and Shrimp Creole

SERVES
6

1 pound boneless, skinless chicken thighs

1 red bell pepper, chopped

1 large onion, peeled and chopped

1 celery stalk, diced

1 (15-ounce) can stewed tomatoes, undrained and chopped

1 clove garlic, peeled and minced

1 tablespoon honey

2 teaspoons ground black pepper

1¼ teaspoons dried oregano

1¼ teaspoons dried thyme

1 teaspoon paprika

1 teaspoon garlic powder

1 teaspoon ground cayenne powder

1 pound of large or jumbo shrimp, peeled, deveined, and cleaned

1 tablespoon lemon juice

1 teaspoon lime juice

1. Place chicken in a 4.5-quart slow cooker, along with all other ingredients except the shrimp and citrus juices.
2. Cover and cook on low for 7–9 hours or on high for 3–4 hours.
3. Add shrimp, lemon and lime juices, cover, and cook on low for 45 minutes–1 hour.

Chicken Taco Filling

1 small onion, peeled and diced

1 clove garlic, peeled and minced

2 tablespoons minced jalapeño pepper

½ pound ground chicken

½ cup diced tomato

½ teaspoon ground chipotle powder

½ teaspoon dried oregano

¼ teaspoon hot paprika

½ teaspoon hot Mexican-style chili powder

½ teaspoon ground cayenne powder

1. In a small nonstick skillet, sauté the onions, garlic, jalapeño, and chicken until the chicken is cooked through, about 3 minutes. Drain off any grease.

2. Add the chicken mixture and the remaining ingredients to a 1.5- to 2-quart slow cooker. Stir to incorporate the spices into the meat. Cook for 6–8 hours on low.

Slow Cooker Suggestions

Chipotle peppers are smoked jalapeño peppers. Their smoky hot flavor is perfect for adding depth and heat to slow-cooked foods. Chipotles are often found as a ground spice or in adobo, a tomato-onion sauce. They are also available as whole, dried peppers.

Enchilada Filling, Paleo Style

3 jalapeño peppers, halved

1 teaspoon canola oil

1 large onion, peeled and diced

3 cloves garlic, peeled and minced

1 teaspoon dried oregano

1 teaspoon ground cayenne powder

½ teaspoon cumin powder

1 (28-ounce) can crushed tomatoes

¾ cup Chicken Stock (see recipe in Chapter 2)

1 tablespoon lime juice

4 cups shredded cooked chicken

1. Place the jalapeño peppers cut side down on a broiler pan. Broil on low for 2 minutes or until they start to brown. Allow to cool, and then dice.

2. In a nonstick skillet, heat the oil over medium heat. Add the onions, garlic, and jalapeño peppers, and sauté until the onions are soft, about 5 minutes.

3. Add the onion mixture to a 4-quart slow cooker. Add the remaining spices, crushed tomatoes, stock, and lime juice. Cook on low for 5–6 hours, then add the shredded meat. Turn up to high and cook for an additional hour.

Slow Cooker Suggestions

Leave at least an inch of headroom in the slow cooker. The lid needs to fit tightly for the slow cooker to cook properly; otherwise the liquid ingredients may boil over, leaving you with a potentially dangerous situation and quite a mess.

Salsa Chicken

4 boneless, skinless chicken breasts

1 (12-ounce) jar mild salsa

Add chicken and salsa to a greased 2.5- or 4-quart slow cooker. Cook on high for 3–4 hours or on low for 6–8 hours.

Slow Cooker Suggestions

Use spaghetti sauce, taco sauce, pizza sauce, or jarred pesto in place of the salsa. Use whatever sauce you like to create a super-easy chicken dish with flavors you love.

Chili Beer Chicken

3 pounds chicken

½ cup flour

1 teaspoon salt, divided

½ teaspoon pepper

2 onions, divided

6 tablespoons butter

1 bottle beer

1 cup tomato sauce

½ teaspoon chili powder

1. Cut the chicken into serving-size pieces. Coat the chicken pieces in a mixture of the flour, ½ teaspoon salt, and pepper.
2. Peel and slice the onions. Sauté the chicken pieces and half of the sliced onions in butter in a pan over medium heat until the chicken is browned.
3. Arrange the chicken mixture and the remaining uncooked onions in the slow cooker.
4. Mix the beer, tomato sauce, chili powder, and remaining ½ teaspoon salt in a medium-size bowl; pour the mixture over the chicken and onions.
5. Cover and heat on low for 3–4 hours.

CHAPTER 9

Asian-Inspired Dishes

104 Teriyaki Chicken

104 Coconut Mango Spiced Chicken

105 Curried Chicken in Coconut Milk

105 Curried Coconut Chicken with Rice

106 Thai Curried Chicken

107 Thai-Influenced Braised Chicken Thighs

107 Thai Peanut Chicken

108 Ginger Caramelized Chicken

109 Orange Chicken

110 Chicken with Mango-Lime Sauce

110 Chicken in Plum Sauce

111 Almond Chicken

112 Asian-Spiced Chicken Breast

112 Almond Chicken Spinach Rolls

Teriyaki Chicken

SERVES **6**

2 pounds boneless, skinless chicken breast

1 (16-ounce) bag frozen stir-fry mixed vegetables, thawed

¼ cup Chicken Broth (see recipe in Chapter 2)

1 cup teriyaki sauce

Cut the chicken breasts into strips or bite-sized pieces. Add to the slow cooker along with the vegetables, broth, and sauce. Stir to mix. Cover and cook on low for 6 hours.

Coconut Mango Spiced Chicken

SERVES **4**

1 (13.5-ounce) can coconut milk

1 large, softball-sized (firm) mango, peeled and cut into cubes (save mango pit)

1 pound boneless, skinless chicken breast, cut into cubes

1 tablespoon dried paprika flakes

1. Pour coconut milk into a 4-quart slow cooker.
2. Place the cubes of mango into the slow cooker, along with the pit of the mango. Add the chicken and paprika flakes. Stir well.
3. Cook on high for 3 hours or on low for 5–6 hours. Remove mango pit before serving.

Curried Chicken in Coconut Milk

SERVES 4

1 small onion, peeled and diced

2 cloves garlic, peeled and minced

1½ tablespoons curry powder

1 cup coconut milk

¾ teaspoon chicken broth base

8 chicken thighs, skin removed

1. Add the onion, garlic, curry powder, coconut milk, and broth base to a 4-quart slow cooker. Stir to mix.
2. Add the chicken thighs. Cover and cook on low for 6 hours.
3. Use a slotted spoon to remove the thighs to a serving bowl. Whisk to combine the sauce and pour over the chicken.

Curried Coconut Chicken with Rice

SERVES 4

4 boneless, skinless chicken breasts

1 (13.5-ounce) can coconut milk

½ teaspoon salt

½ teaspoon ground black pepper

2 teaspoons curry powder

½ teaspoon ground ginger

1 cup brown rice, uncooked

1. Place chicken breasts in a greased 4-quart slow cooker.
2. In a small bowl mix together coconut milk, salt, pepper, curry powder, and ginger. Pour over chicken in slow cooker.
3. Cook on high for 3 hours or on low for 6 hours. Stir in brown rice an hour before serving.

Slow Cooker Suggestions

For weeknight meals many people shy away from cooking whole-grain brown rice because it must be watched closely when cooked on the stove and can take a long time. With a slow cooker you simply stir in brown rice in the last hour of cooking. The rice will turn out light and fluffy with little effort.

Thai Curried Chicken

2½ pounds boneless, skinless chicken breast, cut into 1" cubes

½ cup Thai green curry paste

2¼ cups coconut milk

24 ounces broccoli florets

12 ounces cremini mushrooms, cleaned and sliced

3 tablespoons fish sauce

½ cup honey

Juice of 1 lime

½ cup chopped fresh basil leaves

2 teaspoons almond meal

2 tablespoons water

1. In a 6-quart slow cooker, place the chicken, curry paste, and coconut milk. Stir to combine. Cover and cook on low for 4 hours.
2. Turn the cooker on high, and add the broccoli and mushrooms.
3. In a separate bowl, whisk together the fish sauce, honey, and lime juice, and add this mixture to the slow cooker. Cover and cook for 30 minutes, then uncover and cook for 30 minutes more.
4. Stir in the basil.
5. In a separate bowl, whisk the almond meal with 2 tablespoons of water, and add this mixture to the slow cooker. Stir, and cook for an additional 15–30 minutes, until the liquid has thickened slightly.
6. Serve hot, or rolled up in a lettuce leaf.

Thai-Influenced Braised Chicken Thighs

4 boneless, skinless chicken thighs

3 tablespoons fish sauce

3 tablespoons soy sauce

3 tablespoons lime juice

1" knob galangal root, minced

1" knob ginger, peeled and minced

1 shallot, peeled and thinly sliced

2 cloves garlic, peeled and thinly sliced

¼ teaspoon ground white pepper

Place all ingredients into a 4-quart slow cooker. Cook on high for 2½ hours. Discard the cooking liquid before serving.

Thai Peanut Chicken

1 pound boneless, skinless chicken breast, cubed

2 cups broccoli florets

1 cup Chicken Stock (see recipe in Chapter 2)

¼ cup coarsely chopped peanuts

3 tablespoons soy sauce

2 tablespoons minced Thai bird pepper

2 tablespoons minced garlic

2 tablespoons peeled and minced fresh ginger

¼ cup diced green onions

1. Place the chicken, broccoli, stock, peanuts, soy sauce, pepper, garlic, and ginger into a 4-quart slow cooker. Stir.
2. Cook on low for 4–5 hours or until the chicken is thoroughly cooked. Stir in the green onions prior to serving.

Ginger Caramelized Chicken

1 pound boneless, skinless chicken breast

1 teaspoon canola oil

2 cloves garlic, peeled and minced

2 tablespoons peeled and minced fresh ginger

2 Thai bird peppers, minced

1 shallot, peeled and minced

2 tablespoons fish sauce

1 tablespoon caramel syrup (see recipe in sidebar)

¼ cup Chicken Stock (see recipe in Chapter 2)

1. Cut the chicken breast into 1"-wide strips. Heat the oil in a nonstick skillet. Add the chicken, garlic, ginger, peppers, and shallot. Sauté until the onions and garlic are fragrant.

2. Add the mixture to a 4-quart slow cooker. Add the remaining ingredients, and stir. Cook for 4–5 hours on low.

Slow Cooker Suggestions

To make homemade caramel syrup, place ⅔ cup sugar and ¼ cup water in a large, heavy-bottomed saucepan. Bring to a boil and continue to boil for 10–15 minutes. When the caramel reaches 180°F, remove it from the heat and allow it to cool to room temperature. Store refrigerated in an airtight container.

Orange Chicken

Nonstick spray

3 pounds boneless, skinless chicken breast

1 small onion, peeled and diced

½ cup orange juice

3 tablespoons orange marmalade

1 tablespoon brown sugar

1 tablespoon apple cider vinegar

1 tablespoon gluten-free Worcestershire sauce

1 teaspoon Dijon mustard

1 tablespoon cornstarch mixed with 2 tablespoons hot water

2 tablespoons grated orange zest

1. Grease the slow cooker with nonstick cooking spray. Cut the chicken breast into bite-sized pieces. Add the chicken and the onion to the slow cooker.

2. In a small bowl, mix together the orange juice, marmalade, brown sugar, vinegar, Worcestershire sauce, and mustard. Pour over the chicken in the slow cooker.

3. Cover and cook on low for 5–6 hours, or until chicken is cooked through. About 10 minutes before serving whisk in the cornstarch slurry. Uncover the slow cooker, turn the temperature to high and continue to cook for 10 minutes to thicken the sauce. Serve with orange zest sprinkled on top.

Chicken with Mango-Lime Sauce

SERVES 4

4 boneless, skinless chicken breasts

⅓ cup lime juice

3 tablespoons orange juice

1 large mango, peeled and diced

2 cups gluten-free pasta, cooked

1. Add all ingredients to a greased 4-quart slow cooker. Cook on high for 3–4 hours or on low for 6–8 hours.
2. Serve chicken and sauce over gluten-free pasta.

Slow Cooker Suggestions

Many grocery stores now carry precut mangoes either in the produce section or in the freezer section. Use 1 cup of prepared chopped mango in place of fresh mango if you'd like.

Chicken in Plum Sauce

SERVES 4

Nonstick spray

1¾ cups plum sauce

2 tablespoons butter, melted

2 tablespoons orange juice concentrate, thawed

1 teaspoon Chinese five-spice powder

8 bone-in chicken thighs, skin removed

1. Grease a 4-quart slow cooker with nonstick cooking spray. Add the plum sauce, butter, juice concentrate, and five-spice powder to the slow cooker; stir to combine.
2. Add the chicken thighs. Cover and cook on low for 6 hours or on high for 3 hours.

Almond Chicken

1 (14.5-ounce) can chicken broth

4 strips bacon, cooked

2 pounds boneless, skinless chicken breast

¼ cup dried minced onion

1 (4-ounce) can sliced mushrooms, drained

2 tablespoons gluten-free soy sauce

1½ cups sliced celery

2 cups cooked white rice

1 cup toasted slivered almonds

1. Add the chicken broth to a greased 4-quart slow cooker.
2. Cut the bacon and chicken into bite-sized pieces; add to the slow cooker along with the onion, mushrooms, soy sauce, and celery. Stir to combine.
3. Cover and cook on low for 6 hours.
4. Serve over rice and top with almonds.

Slow Cooker Suggestions

You can toast slivered almonds by adding them to a dry skillet over medium heat. Stir frequently for about 5 minutes until the almonds begin to brown. Alternatively, you can bake them at 400°F for about 5 minutes, stirring them occasionally. Whichever method you use, watch the almonds carefully because they quickly go from toasted to burnt.

Asian-Spiced Chicken Breast

½ cup orange marmalade

1 tablespoon peeled and grated fresh ginger

1 clove garlic, peeled and minced

½ teaspoon Chinese five-spice powder

¼ teaspoon salt

¼ teaspoon freshly ground black pepper

¼ cup orange juice

3 pounds chicken breast

Add the marmalade, ginger, garlic, spice powder, salt, pepper, and orange juice to the slow cooker. Stir to mix. Place the chicken breasts into the cooker. Spoon some of the sauce over the meat. Cover and cook on low for 8 hours or until the internal temperature of the meat is 170°F.

Almond Chicken Spinach Rolls

1 pound boneless, skinless chicken breast

½ cup almonds

2 eggs

2 tablespoons soy sauce

30 large spinach leaves

½ cup white wine

1 cup water

1. Mince the chicken and almonds. Beat the eggs and stir in the chicken, almonds, and soy sauce.

2. Clean the spinach leaves. Place a teaspoon of the chicken mixture on each leaf. Fold the leaves over the chicken mixture, forming a roll, and tie with cotton string.

3. Arrange the rolls on a rack in the slow cooker. Pour the wine and water around the base.

4. Cover and cook on a high setting for 2–3 hours.

CHAPTER 10

Indian-Inspired Dishes

114 Chicken Makhani

115 Goan Chicken Curry

115 "Teekha" Peanut Chicken

116 Chicken Tikka Masala

117 Almond-Flavored Chicken (Badami Murgh)

118 Chicken Curry with Red Potatoes

119 Chicken in a Creamy Sauce (Murgh Korma)

120 Chili Coconut Chicken (Mangalorian Murgh Gassi)

121 Coriander Chicken (Dhaniye Wala Murgh)

122 Fenugreek-Flavored Chicken (Murgh Methiwala)

123 Ginger-Flavored Chicken Curry (Murgh Adraki)

124 Garlic Chicken (Lehsun Wala)

125 Chicken with Pickling Spices (Murgh Achari)

126 Murgh Musallam

127 Slow Cooker Tandoori Chicken

128 Spiced Chicken in Green Curry (Murgh Hariyali)

129 Indian Chicken with Chickpea Sauce

Chicken Makhani

1 pound boneless, skinless chicken breast, cut into chunks

2 shallots, peeled and minced

2 cloves garlic, peeled and minced

½" knob ginger, peeled and minced

2 tablespoons lemon juice

2 teaspoons garam masala

1 teaspoon ground cumin powder

½ teaspoon ground cayenne powder

½ teaspoon ground cloves

½ teaspoon ground fenugreek powder

¼ teaspoon salt

½ teaspoon freshly ground black pepper

1 tablespoon butter

1 tablespoon tomato paste

¾ cup fat-free Greek yogurt

1. Place the chicken, shallots, garlic, ginger, lemon juice, the spices, butter, and tomato paste into a 4-quart slow cooker. Stir. Cook on low for 5 hours.

2. Stir in the yogurt. Serve immediately.

Slow Cooker Suggestions

Greek yogurt is super-thick and creamy but low in fat. It is available in many grocery stores but can be tricky to find in some areas. A reasonable facsimile can be made by lining a colander with cheesecloth and straining low-fat regular yogurt overnight. Be sure to start with twice as much yogurt as the final product should be because the yogurt will reduce by half.

Goan Chicken Curry

1 teaspoon canola oil

2 medium onions, peeled and diced

4 cloves garlic, peeled and minced

3 pounds boneless, skinless chicken thighs, cubed

1 tablespoon peeled and minced fresh ginger

2 cups toasted unsweetened coconut

1 teaspoon ground cinnamon

¼ teaspoon ground nutmeg

½ teaspoon ground cloves

½ teaspoon salt

1 teaspoon cumin seeds

1 teaspoon black mustard seeds

2 tablespoons red pepper flakes

1½ cups water

1. In a large nonstick skillet, heat the oil. Sauté the onions and garlic for 3 minutes.

2. Place all ingredients in a 6-quart slow cooker. Stir. Cover and cook for 6–8 hours on low. Stir before serving.

"Teekha" Peanut Chicken

1 pound boneless, skinless chicken breast, cubed

2 cups broccoli florets

1 cup Chicken Stock (see recipe in Chapter 2)

¼ cup coarsely chopped peanuts

3 tablespoons chili-garlic paste

2 tablespoons minced Thai green chili

2 tablespoons peeled and minced fresh ginger

¼ cup peeled and diced onions

1. Place the chicken, broccoli, Chicken Stock, peanuts, chili-garlic paste, chili, and ginger into a 4-quart slow cooker. Stir.

2. Cook on low for 4–5 hours or until the chicken is thoroughly cooked. Stir in the onions right before serving.

Chicken Tikka Masala

SERVES
4

1 teaspoon Kashmiri red pepper powder

1 tablespoon plus 1½ teaspoons ginger-garlic paste

1 tablespoon plus 1½ teaspoons coriander powder

2 teaspoons garam masala

½ cup yogurt

1½ teaspoons lemon juice

½ teaspoon red food color

4 boneless, skinless chicken thighs (cut into cubes)

1½ tablespoons olive oil, plus more for brushing chicken

1 (14.5-ounce) can diced tomatoes (puréed)

1 tablespoon onion powder

1½ teaspoons ground black pepper

1 teaspoon powdered fennel seeds

½ cup heavy cream

¼ teaspoon salt

1 teaspoon chopped fresh cilantro, for garnish

1. In a large bowl, add the Kashmiri red pepper powder, ginger-garlic paste, coriander powder, garam masala, yogurt, lemon juice, red food color, and chicken and mix well. Cover the bowl and let it sit in the refrigerator for at least 1 hour.

2. Thread the chicken pieces onto skewers. Brush lightly with oil. Grill the skewered chicken until done or place it into the oven for 15–20 minutes at a temperature of 400°F. When cooked, set the grilled chicken tikkas aside.

3. Combine the rest of the ingredients (except for the heavy cream, salt, and cilantro) together in a slow cooker. Cover and cook on high for 1½ hours or on low for 3 hours, letting the masala simmer into a thicker sauce.

4. During the last 45 minutes of cooking, add the heavy cream and stir in the chicken tikka. Adjust salt and add up to ¾ cup water, if necessary. Stir everything together well and continue cooking for 45 minutes.

5. Garnish with cilantro and serve hot.

Almond-Flavored Chicken (Badami Murgh)

¼ cup blanched almonds

Water, as needed

4 tablespoons vegetable oil

1 bay leaf

2 cloves

5 peppercorns

1 green chili, seeded and minced

1 tablespoon ginger-garlic paste

8 pieces skinless, bone-in chicken thighs

½ teaspoon red chili powder

¼ teaspoon turmeric powder

1 teaspoon coriander powder

½ teaspoon garam masala

¼ teaspoon salt

¼ cup plain yogurt, whipped

¼ cup heavy cream

1. In a blender or food processor, blend the almonds with a few tablespoons of water to make a thick, smooth paste. Set aside.

2. In a large pan, heat the vegetable oil over medium heat. Add the bay leaf, cloves, peppercorns, green chili, and ginger-garlic paste. Sauté for about 10 seconds. Add the chicken and sauté for 2–3 minutes.

3. Add the red chili powder, turmeric, coriander, garam masala, and salt; transfer into the slow cooker. Cover and cook on high for 2–3 hours, or on low for 5–6 hours, or until the chicken is cooked through.

4. Toward the last 45 minutes, add the yogurt and up to ½ cup of water, if needed. Cover and continue cooking. Stir occasionally, adding a few tablespoons of water if the dish seems too dry.

5. Toward the last 15 minutes, add the almond paste and the cream. Serve hot.

Chicken Curry with Red Potatoes

1 tablespoon Madras curry powder

1 teaspoon ground allspice

½ teaspoon ground cloves

½ teaspoon ground nutmeg

1 teaspoon ground ginger

2 pounds boneless, skinless chicken thighs, cubed

1 tablespoon canola oil, plus 1 teaspoon

1 onion, peeled and chopped

2 cloves garlic, peeled and chopped

2 jalapeño peppers, chopped

½ pound red potatoes, cubed

⅓ cup light coconut milk

1. In a medium bowl, whisk together the curry powder, allspice, cloves, nutmeg, and ginger. Add the chicken and toss to coat each piece evenly.

2. Heat 1 tablespoon oil in a nonstick skillet. Place the chicken in the skillet and quickly sauté until the chicken starts to brown. Add to a 4-quart slow cooker along with the remaining spice mixture.

3. Heat 1 teaspoon oil in a nonstick skillet and sauté the onions, garlic, and jalapeños until fragrant. Add to the slow cooker.

4. Add the potatoes and coconut milk to the slow cooker. Stir. Cook 7–8 hours on low.

Chicken in a Creamy Sauce (Murgh Korma)

3 tablespoons unsalted cashew nuts, soaked in water for 10 minutes

2 tablespoons white poppy seeds, soaked in water for 20 minutes

2 tablespoons almonds, blanched

Water, as needed

3 tablespoons butter

1 teaspoon cumin powder

2 (1") cinnamon sticks

2 black cardamom pods, bruised

1 large bay leaf

4 cloves

2 green cardamom pods, bruised

¾ cup curry paste

¼ teaspoon salt

1½ pounds boneless diced chicken

1 cup plain yogurt, whipped

1 teaspoon garam masala

Roasted cumin seeds, for garnish

1. Process or blend together the cashew nuts, poppy seeds, almonds, and just enough water to make a smooth, thick paste. Set aside.

2. In a deep pan, heat the butter over medium heat. Add the cumin, cinnamon sticks, black cardamom, bay leaf, cloves, and green cardamom; sauté until fragrant, about 1½ minutes. Add the curry paste and salt. Cook for 1 minute as the butter separates from the curry paste (this indicates that the paste is cooked).

3. Add the chicken; cook for 3–5 minutes. Transfer the contents to the slow cooker. Cover and cook on high for 2½–3 hours or on low for 5–6 hours. You can add up to ½ cup of water if the gravy is too thick.

4. During the last 45 minutes of cooking, add the yogurt and the nut paste and continue cooking.

5. Once the chicken is cooked, add the garam masala. Garnish with roasted cumin seeds and serve hot.

Chili Coconut Chicken (Mangalorian Murgh Gassi)

½ teaspoon black mustard seeds

½ teaspoon cumin seeds

½ teaspoon coriander seeds

3 tablespoons vegetable oil

8 curry leaves

2 medium-sized red onions, peeled and finely chopped

2 teaspoons ginger-garlic paste

3 dried red chilies, roughly pounded

½ teaspoon turmeric powder

¼ teaspoon salt

1½ pounds boneless, skinless chicken, cubed

Water, as needed

1 cup light coconut milk

1. In a small skillet over medium heat, dry-roast the mustard seeds, cumin seeds, and coriander seeds. When the spices release their aroma, remove from heat and let cool. In a spice grinder, grind to a coarse powder. Set aside.

2. In a large skillet, heat the oil over medium heat. Add the curry leaves and the onions; sauté for about 1 minute.

3. Add the ginger-garlic paste and red chilies. Sauté over medium heat until the onions are well browned and the oil begins to separate from the sides of the onion mixture, about 8 minutes. (You can also use ½ cup curry paste, but the results would be slightly different because of the strong flavor of the garam masala in curry paste.)

4. Add the ground spices, turmeric powder, and salt; sauté for 1 minute.

5. Add the chicken pieces; mix well and transfer into a 3- to 4-quart slow cooker. You can add up to ¼ cup of water, although not necessary. Cover and cook on high for 2–3 hours, or on low for 4–6 hours, or until the chicken is cooked through.

6. During the last 30 minutes, add the coconut milk and simmer. Serve hot.

Coriander Chicken (Dhaniye Wala Murgh)

4 tablespoons vegetable oil

2 cloves

2 green cardamom pods

1 (1") cinnamon stick

2 teaspoons ginger-garlic paste

8 skinless chicken thighs

1½ medium tomatoes, finely chopped

½ teaspoon red chili powder

¼ teaspoon salt

2 tablespoons coriander powder

Water, as needed

½ cup plain yogurt, whipped

1 cup minced fresh cilantro leaves

1. In a large pan, heat the vegetable oil over medium heat. Add the cloves, cardamom, and cinnamon. When they begin to sizzle, add the ginger-garlic paste and sauté for about 15 seconds.

2. Add the spice mixture, chicken, and the remaining ingredients, except for the yogurt and cilantro, to a slow cooker. Cover and cook on high for 2½–3 hours, or on low for 5–6 hours, or until the chicken is cooked through.

3. During the last 45 minutes of cooking, add the yogurt and mix well. Cover and continue cooking.

4. Turn the heat off. Add the cilantro leaves and mix well. Put the lid back on and let it stay covered for 10 minutes before serving.

Fenugreek-Flavored Chicken (Murgh Methiwala)

SERVES
4

4 tablespoons vegetable oil

2 cloves

1 green cardamom pod, bruised

1 (1") cinnamon stick

1 medium-sized red onion, peeled and finely chopped

1 tablespoon ginger-garlic paste

2 tablespoons dried fenugreek leaves

8 skinless chicken thighs

½ teaspoon red chili powder

½ teaspoon turmeric powder

¼ teaspoon salt

1 cup plain yogurt, whipped

Water, as needed

1. In a large skillet, heat the vegetable oil over medium heat. Add the cloves, cardamom, and cinnamon. When they begin to sizzle, add the onions and sauté for about 2–3 minutes.

2. Add the ginger-garlic paste and the dried fenugreek leaves. Sauté until the onions are well browned and the oil begins to separate from the onion mixture, about 3–4 minutes.

3. Add the chicken thighs, red chili powder, turmeric powder, and salt. Mix well. Transfer the contents to the slow cooker. Cover and cook on high for 2–3 hours, or on low for 4–5 hours, or until the chicken is cooked through, stirring occasionally.

4. During the last 30–45 minutes of cooking, stir in the yogurt. Add the water if needed. Cover and simmer until the chicken is tender and cooked through. Serve hot.

Ginger-Flavored Chicken Curry (Murgh Adraki)

SERVES
4

2 tablespoons peeled and grated fresh ginger	8 skinless chicken thighs
1 teaspoon coriander powder	½ teaspoon cumin seeds
1 teaspoon garam masala	1 black cardamom pod
½ teaspoon red chili powder	1 bay leaf
¾ cup plain yogurt, whipped	2 medium-sized fresh tomatoes, puréed
4 tablespoons vegetable oil, divided	¼ teaspoon salt
	Water, as needed

1. In a large bowl or resealable plastic bag, combine the ginger, coriander powder, garam masala, red chili powder, yogurt, and 2 tablespoons of the vegetable oil; mix well. Add the chicken and coat all pieces evenly with the marinade. Set aside.

2. In a large skillet, heat the remaining 2 tablespoons of vegetable oil. Add the cumin seeds, cardamom pod, and bay leaf. When the seeds begin to sizzle, add the tomato purée.

3. Sauté over medium heat until the tomatoes are cooked and the oil begins to separate from the tomato mixture, about 3–4 minutes.

4. Add the chicken and the marinade to the tomato mixture, along with the salt. Transfer to the slow cooker. Add up to ½ cup of water. Cover and cook 2½–3 hours, or on low for 5–6 hours, or until the chicken is completely cooked and the juices run clear. Stir occasionally. If you like a thinner gravy, add some more water. Remove the black cardamom pod and bay leaf before serving. Serve hot.

Slow Cooker Suggestions

Indian cooking uses peanut, vegetable, mustard, sesame, and corn oil for cooking. There are 2 varieties of ghee that are used, vanaspathi (vegetable) and usli (clarified butter). Indian cooking does not use any animal fat or lard as a cooking medium.

Garlic Chicken (Lehsun Wala)

1 teaspoon peeled and grated fresh ginger

2 Thai green chilies

15 cloves garlic, peeled

½ tablespoon lemon juice

¼ teaspoon salt

6 whole cloves

2 whole cardamom pods

3 tablespoons olive oil

1½ cups peeled and thinly sliced red onion

1 pound chicken, cut into 2" pieces

½ teaspoon turmeric powder

¼ cup yogurt

1. Make a paste of the ginger, chilies, and about 10–12 cloves of garlic in a blender. Add the lemon juice and mix. Add salt. Set the paste aside. Smash the rest of the garlic cloves with a knife or between your palms. Set aside.

2. Add cloves and cardamom, along with the smashed garlic to a cool skillet. Pour in the olive oil and turn the heat to medium. (Slow heating of the pan infuses the olive oil beautifully with the flavor of garlic and cloves, which will be so distinct in your chicken.)

3. When the oil is hot enough, add the onion. Let it sauté until golden. Transfer the contents, along with the ginger paste prepared earlier, to the slow cooker. Add the chicken and the turmeric into the slow cooker. Stir well. Cover and cook on high for 3–4 hours or on low for 6–7 hours.

4. During the last 45 minutes of cooking, stir in the yogurt. Continue cooking until the chicken is cooked through. Serve hot.

Slow Cooker Suggestions

If you need to cook the chicken longer than the suggested 6–7 hours, add ¼ cup chicken broth to the slow cooker at the beginning of the cooking time. This will help keep the chicken juicy. Alternately, add half an onion.

Chicken with Pickling Spices (Murgh Achari)

SERVES 4

2 tablespoons vegetable oil

½ teaspoon black mustard seeds

½ teaspoon wild fennel seeds (nigella seeds)

2 dried red chilies

¼ teaspoon fenugreek seeds

1 tablespoon ginger-garlic paste

8 skinless chicken thighs

½ teaspoon red chili powder

¼ teaspoon turmeric powder

¼ teaspoon salt

1 cup plain yogurt

Juice of ½ lemon

1. In a large skillet, heat the oil until almost smoking. Reduce the heat to medium. Quickly add the mustard and nigella seeds, red chilies, and fenugreek seeds. Fry for about 30 seconds or until the seeds start to change color and release their aroma.

2. Add the ginger-garlic paste and sauté for another 10 seconds. Add the chicken and sauté for about 5–6 minutes.

3. Transfer the chicken to the slow cooker. Add the red chili powder, turmeric, and salt. Cover and cook on high for 2 hours or on low for 4 hours.

4. During the last 30 minutes of cooking, add the yogurt and mix well. Prop the lid open by ½" for the steam to escape.

5. Add the lemon juice and cook for 10 more minutes. Serve hot.

Murgh Musallam

1 whole chicken

1 lemon, cut into quarters

6 cloves garlic

1 teaspoon black peppercorn

4 black cardamom pods

1 teaspoon cloves

1 cup curry paste, divided

4 tablespoons butter

3 tomatoes, thickly sliced

1. Stuff cavity of the chicken with lemon wedges, garlic, whole spices, and 1 tablespoon of curry paste.

2. Rub the outside of the bird first with butter and then with 2 tablespoons of curry paste. Set aside.

3. Place the tomatoes in the bottom of the slow cooker insert. Place the chicken on top of the tomatoes and pour the rest of the curry paste on top, followed by the remaining butter.

4. Cook on low for 6–7 hours. Discard the skin and pour the thick sauce on top before serving.

Slow Cooker Tandoori Chicken

¼ cup tandoori masala

½ cup plain yogurt

¼ teaspoon red food coloring

1½ tablespoons ginger-garlic paste

1 tablespoon garam masala

3 tablespoons vegetable oil

¼ teaspoon salt

1 whole chicken, skinned

1½ cups peeled and sliced onion

1. Mix all the ingredients (except for the chicken and onion) together in a bowl, making a thick, brightly colored marinade. Make a few incisions in the chicken and rub the marinade all over the chicken. If there is some marinade left, pour it inside the cavity of the bird. Tuck the bird tight. (Place the loose ends of its legs and wings inside to prevent it from burning during the prolonged cooking process.)

2. Add the onion to the slow cooker forming a bottom layer. Place the chicken on top of the onion. Cover and cook on high for the first 1½ hours. Then reduce the heat to low and continue cooking for 4–5 hours or until the chicken is cooked through.

3. Cooking time will depend on the size of the chicken. Cut through the meatier part of the bird and if the juice comes out clear, then the chicken is cooked. Serve hot.

Spiced Chicken in Green Curry (Murgh Hariyali)

3 tablespoons vegetable oil

1 large onion, peeled and minced

2 teaspoons ginger-garlic paste

2 green chilies, seeded and minced

4 tablespoons minced fresh cilantro leaves

4 tablespoons minced fresh mint leaves

5 tablespoons minced spinach leaves

1½ pounds skinless, boneless chicken chunks (preferably thighs)

¼ teaspoon salt

¼ teaspoon red chili powder

Water, as needed

½ cup heavy cream

1. In a large pan, heat the vegetable oil over medium heat. Add the onions and sauté until well browned, about 7–8 minutes. Add the ginger-garlic paste and sauté for 1 minute.

2. Add the green chilies, cilantro, mint, and spinach; fry for about 4–5 minutes. Add the chicken, salt, and red chili powder. Stir well together.

3. Transfer the contents to the slow cooker. Add up to ½ cup of water if needed. Cover and cook on high for 2½–3 hours, or on low for 5–6 hours, or until the chicken is cooked through.

4. During the last 30 minutes of cooking, add the cream and continue cooking. Serve hot.

Slow Cooker Suggestions

Here is another dish that uses mint: Dry fresh mint (or use dried mint leaves) and crush it. Create a marinade of the mint, red chili powder, salt, pepper, and vegetable oil. Add chicken to the marinade and let it marinate for at least 4 hours. Grill or roast in an oven. Simple yet flavorful.

Indian Chicken with Chickpea Sauce

SERVES 4

Nonstick spray

1 tablespoon olive oil

2 medium onions, peeled and finely chopped

3 cloves garlic, peeled and minced

1 teaspoon ground ginger

½ teaspoon turmeric powder

2 teaspoons sweet paprika

2 teaspoons curry powder

1 (14.5-ounce) can low-sodium chicken broth

1 (15–16-ounce) can chickpeas, drained and rinsed

⅓ cup packed fresh cilantro leaves, coarsely chopped

4 boneless, skinless chicken breasts

Hot cooked rice

1. Spray the inside of a 4- or 5-quart slow cooker with nonstick spray.

2. Heat the oil over medium-high heat in a large skillet. When hot, add the onions and cook, stirring frequently, for about 5 minutes or until they begin to brown.

3. Add the garlic, ginger, turmeric, paprika, and curry powder; stir continuously for 1 minute or until fragrant. Add the chicken broth, and chickpeas; bring the mixture to a boil.

4. Once the sauce has reached a boil, mash some of the chickpeas with the back of a wooden spoon or potato masher to help thicken sauce. Add the cilantro and remove from the heat.

5. Place the chicken in the prepared cooker. Pour the chickpea mixture over the chicken.

6. Cover and cook on high for 2–3 hours or low for 4–6 hours. If the sauce is too thin, uncover and continue to cook on high for another 30 minutes. Serve over hot cooked rice.

CHAPTER 11

Italian-Inspired Dishes

132 Shortcut Chicken Parmesan

132 Pesto Chicken

133 Chicken Parmesan

133 Chicken Ragu

134 Tomato and Chicken Sausage Sauce

134 Chicken Saltimbocca

135 Cabbage Rollatini

136 Tuscan Chicken

136 Italian Chicken

137 Slow Cooker Chicken with Green Beans

137 Chicken Alfredo Pasta

138 Chicken Pesto Polenta

139 Tuscan Chicken and White Beans

140 Chicken Piccata

141 Chicken Meatball Sun-Dried Tomato Sauce

142 Italian Chicken Meatloaf

Shortcut Chicken Parmesan

SERVES
4

2 pounds boneless, skinless chicken breast

1 (15-ounce) can tomato sauce

1 (4-ounce) can tomato paste

1 tablespoon Italian seasoning

½ teaspoon dried basil

½ teaspoon garlic powder

½ teaspoon salt

½ teaspoon ground black pepper

2 cups shredded mozzarella cheese

½ cup grated Parmesan cheese

1. Place chicken in the bottom of a greased 4-quart slow cooker.

2. In a large bowl mix together tomato sauce, tomato paste, Italian seasoning, basil, garlic powder, salt, and pepper. Pour sauce over chicken. Cook on high for 3–4 hours or on low for 5–6 hours.

3. An hour prior to serving sprinkle cheeses on top of the tomato sauce. Cook for 45 minutes to an hour until cheeses are melted and gooey.

Pesto Chicken

SERVES
4

2 pounds boneless, skinless chicken thighs

4 red potatoes, diced

1 pint cherry tomatoes

½ cup prepared pesto

½ teaspoon ground black pepper

½ teaspoon salt

Place all ingredients in a greased 4-quart slow cooker. Cook on high for 3–4 hours or on low for 6–8 hours until chicken is tender.

Chicken Parmesan

1 large egg

½ cup bread crumbs

½ teaspoon dried basil

½ teaspoon dried oregano

6 (4-ounce) boneless, skinless chicken breast halves

1 tablespoon olive oil

1¾ cups tomato sauce

½ cup shredded mozzarella cheese

2 tablespoons grated Parmesan cheese

¼ cup chopped fresh parsley leaves

1. In a shallow dish, whisk the egg until foamy. In another shallow dish, combine the bread crumbs, basil, and oregano. Dip the chicken pieces in the egg, then into the bread crumb mixture to coat.

2. Heat olive oil in a large skillet until hot but not smoking. Add the chicken and brown for 3 minutes. Flip, and cook for an additional 3 minutes.

3. Place the chicken in a 4- to 5-quart slow cooker. Cover with tomato sauce. Cook on high for 3–4 hours.

4. Sprinkle with cheeses, turn heat to low, and cook for 10 minutes. Remove from slow cooker and garnish with parsley.

Chicken Ragu

1 pound boneless skinless chicken breast, finely chopped

3 shallots, peeled and finely minced

4 cups marinara sauce

2 teaspoons crushed dried rosemary

2 cloves garlic, peeled and minced

½ teaspoon freshly ground black pepper

½ teaspoon dried oregano

Place all of the ingredients into a 4-quart slow cooker. Stir. Cook on low for 4–6 hours. Stir before serving.

Tomato and Chicken Sausage Sauce

4 Italian chicken sausages, sliced

2 tablespoons tomato paste

1 (28-ounce) can crushed tomatoes

3 cloves garlic, peeled and minced

1 onion, peeled and minced

3 tablespoons minced fresh basil leaves

1 tablespoon minced fresh Italian parsley leaves

¼ teaspoon crushed dried rosemary

¼ teaspoon freshly ground black pepper

1. Quickly brown the sausage slices on both sides in a nonstick skillet. Drain any grease. Add the sausages to a 4-quart slow cooker, along with the remaining ingredients. Stir.

2. Cook on low for 8 hours.

Chicken Saltimbocca

4 boneless, skinless chicken breast tenderloins

4 paper-thin slices prosciutto

1½ cups Chicken Broth (see recipe in Chapter 2)

3 tablespoons capote capers

¼ cup minced fresh sage leaves

1. Wrap each tenderloin in prosciutto. Secure with a toothpick if necessary. Place them in a single layer in an oval 4-quart slow cooker.

2. Pour the broth over the chicken. Sprinkle with the capers and sage. Cook on low for 5 hours or until the chicken is fully cooked. Discard the cooking liquid prior to serving.

Cabbage Rollatini

1 tablespoon coconut oil

½ medium onion, peeled and ground in food processor

4 cloves garlic, peeled and ground in food processor

1 teaspoon dried basil

1 teaspoon cumin powder

1 teaspoon dried oregano

½ head cauliflower, ground in food processor

2 pounds ground chicken

½ cup almond flour

1 egg

½ teaspoon garlic powder

1 head green cabbage, leaves separated and heated (in microwave)

1 (26-ounce) jar tomato sauce

1. Heat oil in a large skillet over medium heat. Add the ground onion, garlic, basil, cumin, and oregano and sauté for 2–3 minutes. Remove from heat.
2. In a large bowl, place the cauliflower, meat, almond flour, egg, and garlic powder. Combine thoroughly with your hands or a large spoon. Add in sautéed onion mixture and mix well.
3. Line a 4-quart slow cooker with 2 large cabbage leaves.
4. Scoop ½–¾ cup of the meat filling onto the stem end of the remaining cabbage leaves, and roll each cabbage leaf as tightly as possible.
5. Place rolls in the slow cooker, seam side down. Pour tomato sauce evenly over the top of the cabbage rolls.
6. Cook on high for 4 hours. Serve warm, and spoon sauce and drippings over the rolls.

Tuscan Chicken

SERVES
4

1 pound boneless, skinless chicken breast tenderloins

1 cup Chicken Stock (see recipe in Chapter 2)

4 cloves garlic, peeled and minced

1 shallot, peeled and minced

2 tablespoons lime juice

1 tablespoon lemon juice

1 tablespoon minced fresh rosemary leaves

1. Place all the ingredients into a 4-quart slow cooker. Stir.
2. Cook on low for 4 hours or until the chicken is fully cooked.

Italian Chicken

SERVES
6

6 (5-ounce) boneless, skinless chicken breasts

2 bay leaves

½ teaspoon ground black pepper

½ teaspoon dried oregano

½ teaspoon dried basil

32-ounce jar tomato sauce

1. Add chicken to the bottom of a 4-quart slow cooker and sprinkle seasonings over chicken.
2. Pour sauce over seasoned chicken. Cover the chicken completely with sauce.
3. Cover and cook on low for 6 hours or on high for 3½–4 hours. Serve with an Italian vegetable medley.

Slow Cooker Chicken with Green Beans

SERVES 4

4 boneless, skinless chicken breasts

1 cup gluten-free Italian salad dressing

½ teaspoon salt

1 cup diced green bell peppers

1 cup diced onions

4 potatoes, peeled and quartered

1 (14.5-ounce) can green beans, drained and rinsed

1. Place chicken in a greased 4-quart slow cooker. Add Italian dressing, salt, green peppers, onions, and potatoes.
2. Cook on high for 3 hours or on low for 6 hours.
3. Add green beans during the last hour of cooking.

Chicken Alfredo Pasta

SERVES 4

1 pound boneless, skinless chicken thighs, cut into ¾" pieces

1 (14-ounce) can quartered artichokes, drained

1 (16-ounce) jar gluten-free Alfredo pasta sauce

1 cup water

½ cup sun-dried tomatoes, drained and chopped

8 ounces gluten-free pasta, uncooked

2 tablespoons shredded Parmesan cheese

1. In a greased 4-quart slow cooker, mix chicken, artichokes, Alfredo sauce, and water. Cover and cook on high for 3 hours or on low for 6 hours.
2. Forty-five minutes before serving, stir tomatoes and uncooked pasta into chicken mixture.
3. Cover lid and continue to cook until pasta is al dente. Sprinkle Parmesan cheese over individual servings.

Chicken Pesto Polenta

SERVES 6

4 boneless, skinless chicken breasts, cut into bite-sized pieces

1 cup prepared pesto, divided

1 medium onion, peeled and finely diced

4 cloves garlic, peeled and minced

1½ teaspoons dried Italian seasoning

1 (16-ounce) tube prepared polenta, cut into ½" slices

2 cups chopped fresh spinach leaves

1 (14.5-ounce) can diced tomatoes

1 (8-ounce) bag shredded low-fat Italian cheese blend

1. In a large bowl, combine chicken pieces with ½ cup pesto, onion, garlic, and Italian seasoning.

2. In a greased 4-quart slow cooker, layer half of chicken mixture, half the polenta, half the spinach, and half the tomatoes. Continue to layer, ending with tomatoes. Cover and cook on low for 4–6 hours or on high for 2–3 hours.

3. An hour before serving drizzle remaining pesto over casserole and top with shredded cheese. Cover and continue to cook for 45 minutes to an hour until cheese has melted.

Slow Cooker Suggestions

Instead of using prepared pesto you can easily make your own: In a high-powered blender or food processor add 2 cups fresh basil leaves, ½ cup extra-virgin olive oil, ½ cup Parmesan cheese, ½ cup pine nuts, 3 garlic cloves, and ¼ teaspoon salt and ¼ teaspoon pepper. Blend on high for a few minutes until mixture is creamy. You can use blanched almond flour in place of the Parmesan cheese, if you are intolerant to dairy.

Tuscan Chicken and White Beans

SERVES 4

3 large boneless, skinless chicken breasts

1 (15.5-ounce) can white beans, drained and rinsed

1 (14.5-ounce) can diced tomatoes

1 (4-ounce) can mushrooms, drained

¼ cup Spanish olives stuffed with pimientos, sliced in half

2 teaspoons onion powder

1 teaspoon garlic powder

1 teaspoon dried basil

1 teaspoon dried oregano

1 teaspoon ground black pepper

½ teaspoon salt

2 teaspoons olive oil

2 cups cooked rice, for serving

1. Cut chicken breasts into large chunks and place in a greased 4-quart slow cooker.

2. Add beans, tomatoes (including the juice), mushrooms, and olives. Add onion powder, garlic powder, basil, oregano, ground pepper, and salt.

3. Mix ingredients together in the slow cooker. Drizzle olive oil over the top of the chicken and vegetables.

4. Cook on high for 3½–4 hours or on low for 6 hours. Serve over cooked rice.

Slow Cooker Suggestions

White beans, which are also called navy beans, Boston beans, or Yankee beans, are small, lightly colored beans that are very mild in taste and work well in a variety of recipes. If you don't have white beans available, cannellini beans or northern beans, which are slightly larger, are excellent substitutes.

Chicken Piccata

2 large boneless, skinless chicken breasts, cut into very
    thin slices

1 cup brown rice flour

1 tablespoon olive oil

¼ cup lemon juice

3 tablespoons nonpareil capers

¾ cup Chicken Stock (see recipe in Chapter 2)

¼ teaspoon freshly ground black pepper

1. Dredge both sides of the sliced chicken breasts in the flour. Discard leftover flour.
2. Heat olive oil in a nonstick pan. Quickly sear the chicken on both sides to brown, approximately 1 minute per side.
3. Place the chicken, lemon juice, capers, stock, and pepper into a greased 4-quart slow cooker.
4. Cook on high for 2–3 hours or on low for 4–6 hours until the chicken is cooked through and the sauce has thickened.

Slow Cooker Suggestions

Dredging is a process in which food is dragged through dry ingredients like cornstarch or gluten-free bread crumbs to coat it. Dredging can be a one-step process, but if a thicker crust or coating is desired, the food is dredged in flour once, dipped in egg or milk, then dredged through flour, cornmeal, or gluten-free bread crumbs again. In slow cooking, dredging often has a dual purpose of coating the meat and thickening the sauce.

Chicken Meatball Sun-Dried Tomato Sauce

SERVES
6

1 pound ground chicken

½ cup bread crumbs

1 large egg

2 cloves garlic, peeled and minced

1 shallot, peeled and minced

1 (28-ounce) can crushed tomatoes

½ cup julienne-cut dry (not oil-packed) sun-dried tomatoes

1 medium onion, peeled and minced

1 tablespoon minced fresh basil leaves

1. Preheat the oven to 375°F. Line 2 baking sheets with parchment paper.
2. In a large bowl, use your hands to mix the chicken, bread crumbs, egg, garlic, and shallot. Form into 1" balls. Place on the baking sheets and bake for 15 minutes or until cooked through.
3. Pour the crushed tomatoes into a 4- to 5-quart slow cooker. Add the sun-dried tomatoes, onion, and basil. Stir. Add the meatballs and stir to coat with sauce. Cook on low for 6 hours.

Slow Cooker Suggestions

Despite losing moisture as they are dried, sun-dried tomatoes retain all of the nutritional benefits of fresh tomatoes, making them a good source of vitamin C and lycopene. Their flavor is more concentrated than fresh tomatoes.

Italian Chicken Meatloaf

6 slices toasted Italian bread

½ cup skim milk

2 teaspoons olive oil

3 shallots, peeled and diced

2 cloves garlic, peeled and finely minced

1 pound ground chicken

2 large eggs

1 teaspoon dried basil

1 teaspoon dried oregano

½ teaspoon dried thyme

½ teaspoon hot smoked paprika

½ teaspoon freshly ground black pepper

½ teaspoon kosher salt

1. Soak bread in milk for 1 minute, then squeeze dry. Roughly chop the bread and place in a large bowl.
2. Grease slow cooker with the olive oil.
3. Mix remaining ingredients with the bread. Place meat mixture in the slow cooker and pat out so that it's an even thickness. Cook on low for 4–6 hours. Use a meat thermometer to make sure internal temperature is 170°F. Let sit for 15 minutes and serve.

Slow Cooker Suggestions

It's extremely important to cook poultry to the proper temperature. And in order to do that, an instant-read meat thermometer is a vital kitchen tool. For a meal like this one, make sure that the thermometer is in the thickest part of the meat. However, if you were checking the temperature of a roast chicken, for example, you would place the thermometer in the inner thigh near the breast, but not touching the bone.

CHAPTER 12

Mediterranean-Inspired Dishes

144 Roast Chicken with Lemon and Artichokes

145 Chicken and Artichokes

145 Mediterranean Chicken Casserole

146 Spicy Olive Chicken

147 Sun-Dried Tomato and Feta–Stuffed Chicken

148 Balsamic Chicken and Spinach

148 Chicken Fricassee

149 Rosemary Chicken with Potatoes

150 Sage Ricotta Chicken Breasts

151 Lemony Roast Chicken

152 Chicken Cutlets with Red Onion Sauce

152 Five-Ingredient Greek Chicken

153 Slow-Roasted Chicken with Potatoes, Parsnips, and Onions

154 Chicken Budapest

Roast Chicken with Lemon and Artichokes

Nonstick spray

1 small onion, peeled and quartered

1 large carrot, peeled and sliced

1 large lemon

3 cloves garlic

1 (4-pound) whole chicken

½ teaspoon salt

½ teaspoon freshly ground black pepper

2 tablespoons olive oil

1 (6-ounce) jar marinated artichoke hearts

1. Grease a large 6-quart slow cooker with nonstick cooking spray.
2. Place the onion and carrot in the slow cooker. Cut the lemon in half. Place half of the lemon, along with the garlic cloves, into the cavity of the chicken.
3. Cut the remainder of the lemon into 4–5 large slices.
4. Place the chicken on top of the onions and carrots. Place lemon slices on top of the chicken. Sprinkle salt and pepper over the chicken. Drizzle olive oil over the chicken. Cook on low for 6–8 hours, or on high for 3–4 hours.
5. An hour before serving, place artichokes (discarding the oil) over the top of the chicken.

Slow Cooker Suggestions

Make a sauce using the liquids from the cooked chicken by straining them into a saucepan. Whisk in 2 tablespoons of brown rice flour or garbanzo bean flour and cook on low heat until thickened. The resulting sauce will have a fragrant aroma of lemon, artichokes, and garlic. Serve over rice or gluten-free pasta with green beans or a salad.

Chicken and Artichokes

SERVES
4

8 boneless, skinless chicken thighs

½ cup Chicken Stock (see recipe in Chapter 2)

1 tablespoon fresh lemon juice

2 teaspoons dried thyme

1 clove garlic, peeled and minced

¼ teaspoon freshly ground black pepper

1 (13-ounce) can artichoke hearts, drained

Add all the ingredients to the slow cooker; stir to mix. Cover and cook on low for 6 hours. If necessary, uncover and allow to cook for 30 minutes or more to thicken the sauce.

Mediterranean Chicken Casserole

SERVES
4

1 medium butternut squash, peeled and cut into 2" cubes

1 medium green bell pepper, seeded and diced

1 (14.5-ounce) can diced tomatoes, undrained

4 boneless, skinless chicken breast halves, cut into bite-sized pieces

½ cup mild salsa

¼ cup raisins

¼ teaspoon ground cinnamon

¼ teaspoon cumin powder

2 cups cooked rice, for serving

¼ cup chopped fresh parsley leaves

1. Add squash and bell pepper to the bottom of a greased 4-quart slow cooker. Mix tomatoes, chicken, salsa, raisins, cinnamon, and cumin together and pour on top of squash and peppers.

2. Cover and cook on low for 6 hours or on high for 3 hours, until squash is fork tender.

3. Remove chicken and vegetables from the slow cooker with a slotted spoon. Serve over cooked rice. Ladle remaining sauce from the slow cooker over the vegetables. Garnish with parsley.

Spicy Olive Chicken

1 (3-pound) whole chicken, cut into 8 pieces

1 teaspoon salt

½ teaspoon ground black pepper

4 tablespoons unsalted butter

⅔ cup chopped sweet onion

2 tablespoons capers, drained and rinsed

24 green olives, pitted

½ cup Chicken Broth (see recipe in Chapter 2)

½ cup dry white wine

1 teaspoon prepared Dijon mustard

½ teaspoon hot sauce

2 cups cooked white rice

¼ cup fresh chopped parsley leaves

1. Sprinkle the chicken pieces with salt and pepper and brown them in the butter in a large skillet for about 3 minutes on each side. Sauté the onion in the same skillet for an additional 3–5 minutes. Pour chicken, onions, capers, and olives into a greased 4-quart slow cooker.

2. In a small bowl whisk together the broth, wine, and mustard. Pour over chicken in the slow cooker. Add hot sauce. Cover and cook on high for 3–3½ hours or on low for 5½–6 hours.

3. When ready to serve, place chicken over rice. Ladle sauce and olives over each serving. Garnish with parsley.

Slow Cooker Suggestions

Capers are flavorful berries. Picked green, they can be packed in salt or brine. Try to find the smallest—they seem to have more flavor than the big ones do. Capers are great on their own or incorporated into sauces. They are also good in salads and as a garnish on many dishes that would otherwise be dull.

Sun-Dried Tomato and Feta–Stuffed Chicken

4 boneless, skinless chicken breasts

½ cup chopped oil-packed sun-dried tomatoes

⅓ cup crumbled feta cheese

¼ cup chopped pitted Kalamata olives

1½ cups fresh baby spinach leaves

2 tablespoons olive oil

½ teaspoon salt

½ teaspoon freshly ground black pepper

1. Flatten chicken breasts on a wooden cutting board with the flat side of a meat mallet. Set chicken breasts aside.

2. In a small bowl mix together the tomatoes, cheese, and olives.

3. Place 3–4 spinach leaves in the middle of each flattened chicken breast. Place 2–3 tablespoons of the tomato filling on top of the spinach leaves.

4. Fold one side of the flattened chicken breast over the filling and continue to roll into a cylinder. Secure with 2–3 toothpicks per chicken breast. Place the chicken rolls seam side down in a greased 4-quart slow cooker.

5. Drizzle olive oil evenly over the top of the chicken rolls and sprinkle the chicken with salt and pepper. Cook on high for 3 hours or on low for 6 hours.

Balsamic Chicken and Spinach

SERVES 4

¾ pound boneless, skinless chicken breast, cut into strips

¼ cup balsamic vinegar

4 cloves garlic, peeled and minced

1 tablespoon minced fresh oregano leaves

1 tablespoon minced fresh Italian parsley leaves

½ teaspoon freshly ground black pepper

5 ounces baby spinach leaves

1. Place the chicken, vinegar, garlic, and spices into a 4-quart slow cooker. Stir. Cook on low for 6 hours.

2. Stir in the baby spinach and continue to cook until it starts to wilt, about 15 minutes. Stir before serving.

Chicken Fricassee

SERVES 6

2 cups sliced red cabbage

2 carrots, peeled and cut into coin-sized pieces

2 celery stalks, diced

1 onion, peeled and sliced

3 bone-in chicken breasts

¾ cup Chicken Stock (see recipe in Chapter 2)

2 teaspoons paprika

2 teaspoons dried thyme

2 teaspoons dried parsley

1. Place the cabbage, carrots, celery, and onions on the bottom of an oval 4-quart slow cooker.

2. Place the chicken skin side up on top of the vegetables. Pour the stock over the chicken and sprinkle it evenly with the spices. Pat the spices onto the chicken skin.

3. Cook on low 6 hours or until the chicken is cooked through. Remove the skin prior to serving.

Rosemary Chicken with Potatoes

SERVES 6

1 tablespoon olive oil

2 pounds boneless, skinless chicken thighs

½ teaspoon kosher salt

½ teaspoon freshly ground black pepper

6 small red potatoes, halved

1 leek (white and pale green parts only), sliced into 1" pieces

6 sprigs fresh rosemary, divided

1 garlic clove, peeled and minced

½ cup Chicken Broth (see recipe in Chapter 2)

¼ cup capers

1. Heat the olive oil in a large skillet over medium heat until hot but not smoking. Add chicken, and season with salt and pepper. Cook for 5 minutes on one side and flip. Cook for an additional 5 minutes.
2. Place the potatoes and leek into a 4- to 5-quart slow cooker. Top with 5 sprigs of rosemary and garlic.
3. Place chicken thighs on the rosemary. Pour the broth over the chicken and potatoes.
4. Cover and cook on high for 3–4 hours or until the juices run clear from the chicken. Sprinkle with capers just before serving, and garnish with remaining rosemary.

Sage Ricotta Chicken Breasts

6 fresh sage leaves, chopped

½ cup part-skim ricotta cheese

4 (4-ounce) boneless, skinless chicken breasts

½ teaspoon kosher salt

½ teaspoon freshly ground black pepper

1 tablespoon olive oil

½ cup white wine

¾ cup Chicken Broth (see recipe in Chapter 2)

¼ cup Niçoise olives, pitted and chopped

1. Combine sage and ricotta in a small bowl.
2. Gently slice a slit into a chicken breast to form a pocket. Stuff 2 tablespoons of filling into the chicken. Tie with kitchen twine and trim ends. Repeat with the rest of the chicken and cheese.
3. Season the chicken breasts with salt and pepper. Heat olive oil in a large skillet until it's hot but not smoking. Place chicken in the skillet and sear on one side, about 3 minutes. Flip and brown on the second side, about 3 minutes. Gently place chicken in a 4- to 5-quart slow cooker. Pour wine and Chicken Broth into the slow cooker.
4. Cook on low for 6–8 hours.
5. Cut twine from chicken breasts and sprinkle with olives.

Lemony Roast Chicken

SERVES 6

1 (3½-pound) frying chicken

1 teaspoon kosher salt

1 teaspoon freshly ground black pepper

1 clove garlic, peeled and crushed

3 tablespoons olive oil

2 lemons, quartered

½ cup Chicken Broth (see recipe in Chapter 2)

1. Rinse chicken inside and out and pat dry. Rub with salt, pepper, and garlic. Brush with olive oil.

2. Place lemon quarters in the bottom of a 4- to 5-quart slow cooker. Top with the chicken. Pour the broth over the chicken.

3. Cover and cook on high for 1 hour. Reduce heat to low and cook for 5–6 hours.

4. Insert a meat thermometer into the thickest part of the thigh. The chicken is done when it registers 170°F.

Slow Cooker Suggestions

Once you're done with dinner, place the chicken bones back in the slow cooker. Cover with water, and add in some celery, onion, carrots, dill, and parsley. Cook on low for 10 hours, and you have chicken stock!

Chicken Cutlets with Red Onion Sauce

SERVES 4

4 chicken cutlets

½ teaspoon salt, divided

½ teaspoon ground black pepper, divided

2 tablespoons olive oil

1 large red onion, peeled and thinly sliced

⅓ cup sweetened rice vinegar

1. Season chicken cutlets with ¼ teaspoon salt and ¼ teaspoon pepper and place in a greased 2.5-quart slow cooker.

2. In a small bowl mix together olive oil, red onion, and sweetened rice vinegar. Pour over the chicken cutlets. Cook on high for 3–4 hours or on low for 6–8 hours until chicken is cooked through. Add remaining ¼ teaspoon salt and remaining ¼ teaspoon pepper per serving.

Five-Ingredient Greek Chicken

SERVES 6

6 (5-ounce) bone-in chicken thighs, skinned

½ cup Kalamata olives

1 (6.5-ounce) jar artichokes in olive oil, undrained

1 pint cherry tomatoes

¼ cup chopped fresh parsley leaves

1. Place chicken, olives, artichokes and artichoke oil, and cherry tomatoes in a 4- to 5-quart slow cooker.

2. Cover and cook on low for 4–6 hours. Serve in large bowls garnished with parsley.

Slow-Roasted Chicken with Potatoes, Parsnips, and Onions

SERVES

6

4 medium onions, peeled and sliced

1 (6-pound) roasting chicken

6 large red potatoes, peeled and quartered

4 medium parsnips, peeled and diced

1 teaspoon kosher salt

1 teaspoon ground black pepper

1. Cover the bottom of a 6- to 6.5-quart oval slow cooker with half of the onions.
2. Place the chicken, breast side up, on top of the onions.
3. Cover the chicken with the remaining onions.
4. Arrange the potatoes and parsnips around the chicken and sprinkle with salt and pepper.
5. Cover and cook on low for 8 hours or until the chicken has an internal temperature of 170°F as measured using a food thermometer. Discard the chicken skin before serving.

Slow Cooker Suggestions

Parsnips have a mild flavor and a texture that is well suited to extended cooking times. Always peel off the bitter skin before cooking. If parsnips are not available, carrots are an acceptable substitute.

Chicken Budapest

1 cup plus 2 tablespoons flour, divided

½ teaspoon salt

½ teaspoon ground white pepper

1 (2½-pound) whole chicken

3 tablespoons oil

2 onions, peeled

3 cloves garlic, peeled

3 tablespoons paprika

2½ cups water, divided

2 cups sour cream

1. Mix 1 cup of flour with the salt and pepper. Cut the chicken into serving-sized pieces and coat with the flour mixture. Sauté the chicken pieces in oil in a pan over medium heat until the meat is lightly browned.

2. Slice the onions. Crush and slice the garlic. Add the onions and garlic to the pan with the chicken and stir over medium heat until the onion is soft. Add the paprika to the pan and stir to mix.

3. Add the chicken-and-onion mixture and 2 cups of water to the slow cooker.

4. Cover and heat on a low setting for 4–6 hours.

5. Mix the remaining water and flour in a mixing bowl, then add the sour cream and blend well. An hour before serving, slowly stir the sour cream mixture into the chicken.

CHAPTER 13

International Favorites

156 Caribbean Chicken Curry

157 Spanish Chicken and Rice

158 Peruvian Roast Chicken with Red Potatoes

159 Peruvian Chicken with Aji Verde

160 Chicken with Figs

161 Moroccan Chicken

162 Jerk Chicken

162 Ethiopian Chicken Stew

163 Tarragon Chicken

164 Filipino Chicken Adobo

164 Chicken in Onion Sauce

165 South African–Style Chicken

166 Tamales with Chicken and Olives

Caribbean Chicken Curry

1 tablespoon Madras curry powder

1 teaspoon ground allspice

½ teaspoon ground cloves

½ teaspoon ground nutmeg

1 teaspoon ground ginger

2 pounds boneless, skinless chicken thighs, cubed

1 teaspoon canola oil

1 onion, peeled and chopped

2 cloves garlic, peeled and chopped

2 jalapeño peppers, chopped, seeds removed

½ pound red potatoes, cubed

⅓ cup light coconut milk

1. In a medium bowl, whisk together the curry powder, allspice, cloves, nutmeg, and ginger. Add the chicken and toss to coat each piece evenly.
2. Place the chicken in a nonstick skillet and quickly sauté until the chicken starts to brown. Add to a 4-quart slow cooker along with the remaining spice mixture.
3. Heat the oil in a nonstick skillet and sauté the onion, garlic, and jalapeños until fragrant, about 3–5 minutes. Add to the slow cooker.
4. Add the potatoes and coconut milk to the slow cooker. Stir. Cook 7–8 hours on low.

Spanish Chicken and Rice

1 tablespoon olive oil

4 bone-in chicken thighs

4 bone-in split chicken breasts

2 tablespoons lemon juice

4 ounces smoked ham, cubed

1 medium onion, peeled and diced

1 red bell pepper, seeded and diced

4 cloves garlic, peeled and minced

Nonstick spray

2½ cups water

1¾ cups Chicken Broth (see recipe in Chapter 2)

1 teaspoon dried oregano

½ teaspoon salt

¼ teaspoon saffron threads, crushed

⅛ teaspoon dried red pepper flakes, crushed

2 cups converted long-grain rice, uncooked

1. Bring the oil to temperature in a large nonstick skillet over medium-high heat. Put the chicken pieces in the skillet skin side down and fry for 5 minutes or until the skin is browned. Transfer the chicken to a plate and sprinkle the lemon juice over the chicken.

2. Pour off and discard all but 2 tablespoons of the fat in the skillet. Reduce the heat under the skillet to medium. Add the ham, onion, and bell pepper; sauté for 5 minutes or until the onion is transparent. Stir in the garlic and sauté for 30 seconds.

3. Grease a 6-quart slow cooker with nonstick spray. Pour the cooked ham and vegetables into the slow cooker. Add the water, broth, oregano, salt, saffron, red pepper flakes, and rice. Stir to combine.

4. Place the chicken thighs, skin side up, in the slow cooker and add the breast pieces on top of the thighs. Cover and cook on low for 6 hours or until the rice is tender and the chicken is cooked through. Place a split chicken breast and thigh on each serving plate. Stir and fluff the rice mixture and spoon it onto the plates.

Peruvian Roast Chicken with Red Potatoes

1 (3½-pound) whole chicken

2½ tablespoons garlic powder

2 tablespoons paprika

1½ tablespoons cumin powder

2 teaspoons ground black pepper

1 teaspoon salt

½ teaspoon dried oregano

1 lemon, cut into quarters

2 pounds red potatoes, washed and quartered

4 tablespoons white vinegar

4 tablespoons white wine

2 tablespoons olive oil

1. Loosen skin of the chicken over the breast meat if possible, being careful not to break the skin.
2. In a small bowl mix together the garlic powder, paprika, cumin, black pepper, salt, and oregano. Generously rub the chicken with the spice mixture. Rub the meat of the chicken under the skin with the spice mixture as well. Place the lemon quarters inside the chicken.
3. Place the potatoes in the bottom of a 6-quart slow cooker. Place the spice-rubbed chicken on top of the potatoes.
4. Drizzle the vinegar, wine, and olive oil over the chicken.
5. Cook on high for 4 hours or on low for 8 hours.

Slow Cooker Suggestions

Peruvian chicken is often served with a dipping sauce on the side. You can make a homemade version by mixing together ½ cup mayonnaise with 2 tablespoons yellow mustard and 3 tablespoons lime juice.

Peruvian Chicken with Aji Verde

SERVES 4

5 cloves garlic, peeled and mashed

2 bone-in chicken breasts

2 tablespoons red wine vinegar

1 teaspoon cumin powder

1 teaspoon sugar

2 tablespoons soy sauce

2 jalapeño peppers, chopped

½ cup fresh cilantro leaves

⅓ cup water

⅓ cup Cotija cheese

1 teaspoon apple cider vinegar

¼ teaspoon salt

1. Spread the cloves of garlic over the chicken pieces. Place into an oval 4-quart slow cooker. Pour the vinegar, cumin, sugar, and soy sauce over the chicken. Cook on low for 5 hours or until the chicken is thoroughly cooked.

2. In a food processor, pulse together the jalapeños, cilantro, water, cheese, cider vinegar, and salt.

3. Remove the chicken from the slow cooker. Remove and discard the skin. Spread the sauce on each breast. Return to the slow cooker and cook on low 15 minutes before serving.

Slow Cooker Suggestions

Cotija cheese is a Mexican cheese made from cow's milk. It can be found in large blocks or grated. It has a flavor profile similar to Parmesan and can be rather crumbly. Use it as a topping for salads, tacos, soups, beans, or tostadas.

Chicken with Figs

½ pound boneless, skinless chicken thighs

¾ pound boneless, skinless chicken breast

¾ cup dried figs

1 sweet potato, peeled and diced

1 onion, peeled and chopped

3 cloves garlic, peeled and minced

2 teaspoons cumin powder

1 teaspoon coriander powder

½ teaspoon ground cayenne powder

½ teaspoon ground ginger

½ teaspoon turmeric powder

½ teaspoon ground orange peel

½ teaspoon freshly ground black pepper

2¾ cups Chicken Stock (see recipe in Chapter 2)

¼ cup orange juice

1. Cube the chicken. Quickly sauté the chicken in a dry nonstick skillet until it starts to turn white. Drain off any excess grease.
2. Place the chicken and remaining ingredients into a 4-quart slow cooker. Stir. Cook for 6 hours on low. Stir before serving.

Moroccan Chicken

½ teaspoon coriander powder

½ teaspoon ground cinnamon

¼ teaspoon salt

1 teaspoon cumin powder

3 pounds (about 8) boneless, skinless chicken thighs, diced

1 onion, peeled and thinly sliced

4 cloves garlic, peeled and minced

2 tablespoons minced fresh ginger

½ cup water

4 ounces dried apricots, halved

1 (15-ounce) can chickpeas, drained and rinsed

1. In a large bowl, combine the coriander, cinnamon, salt, and cumin. Toss chicken in the spice mixture.
2. Place onion, garlic, ginger, and water into a 4-quart slow cooker. Place chicken on top of vegetables. Place dried apricots and chickpeas on top of chicken.
3. Cover and cook on low for 5–6 hours.

Jerk Chicken

 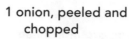

3 pounds boneless, skinless chicken breast

3 tablespoons Jamaican jerk seasoning

1 Scotch bonnet pepper, sliced

¼ cup fresh thyme leaves

½ cup lemon juice

1 onion, peeled and chopped

1 clove garlic, peeled and minced

1 teaspoon hickory liquid smoke

½ teaspoon ground allspice

¼ teaspoon ground cloves

Place the chicken on the bottom of a 6- to 7-quart slow cooker. Pour the remaining ingredients on top. Cook on low for 5 hours.

Ethiopian Chicken Stew

1 (14.5-ounce) can diced tomatoes, undrained

1½ pounds boneless, skinless chicken thighs

¼ cup lemon juice

2 tablespoons coconut butter

3 large onions, peeled and diced

1 tablespoon paprika

1 teaspoon ground ginger

1 teaspoon ground cayenne powder

1 teaspoon turmeric powder

½ teaspoon ground black pepper

2 cups water

8 hard-boiled eggs

1. Place tomatoes into a 6-quart slow cooker. Add the chicken thighs and lemon juice. Add the coconut butter, onions, and all the spices.

2. Add the water. Cover and cook on low for 6–8 hours or on high for 4–5 hours.

3. Ladle into bowls with a peeled hard-boiled egg in each individual bowl.

Tarragon Chicken

½ cup plus 2 tablespoons brown rice flour, divided

½ teaspoon salt

8 bone-in chicken thighs, skin removed

2 tablespoons butter

2 tablespoons olive oil

1 medium yellow onion, peeled and diced

1 cup dry white wine

1 cup Chicken Broth (see recipe in Chapter 2)

1 teaspoon dried tarragon

1 cup heavy cream

1. Add ½ cup flour, salt, and the chicken thighs to a gallon-sized plastic bag; close and shake to coat the chicken.

2. Add the butter and oil to a large sauté pan and bring it to temperature over medium-high heat. Add the chicken thighs; brown the chicken by cooking the pieces on one side for 5 minutes, and then turning them over and frying them for another 5 minutes. Drain the chicken on paper towels and then place in a 4- to 6-quart slow cooker. Cover the slow cooker. Set temperature to low.

3. Add the onion to the sauté pan; sauté until the onion is transparent, about 3–5 minutes. Stir in 2 tablespoons of brown rice flour, cooking until the onion just begins to brown. Slowly pour the wine into the pan, stirring to scrape the browned bits off of the bottom of the pan and into the sauce. Add the broth. Cook and stir for 15 minutes or until the sauce is thickened enough to coat the back of a spoon. Stir the tarragon into the sauce, and then pour the sauce over the chicken in the slow cooker. Cover and cook for 3 hours on high or 6 hours on low.

4. Pour the cream into the slow cooker; cover and cook for an additional 15 minutes or until the cream is heated through. Serve immediately.

Slow Cooker Suggestions

After 3 hours on high, the chicken will be cooked through and ready to eat. Yet, if you prefer to leave the chicken cooking for a longer period, after 7–8 hours on low the meat will be tender enough to fall away from the bone. You can then remove the bones before you stir in the cream.

Filipino Chicken Adobo

2 boneless, skinless chicken thighs

¼ cup water

¼ cup cane vinegar

¼ cup soy sauce

1 teaspoon whole black peppercorns

5 cloves garlic, peeled and halved

2 bay leaves

Place all ingredients in a 2-quart slow cooker. Cook for 6–8 hours. Discard the bay leaves before serving.

Chicken in Onion Sauce

SERVES

8

5 large onions, peeled and thinly sliced

4 cloves garlic, peeled and minced

¼ cup fresh lemon juice

1 teaspoon salt

¼ teaspoon ground cayenne powder

4 chicken thighs, skin removed

¼ teaspoon freshly ground black pepper

1. Add the onions, garlic, lemon juice, salt, and cayenne powder to the slow cooker; stir to combine. Nestle the chicken legs into the onion mixture. Cover and cook on low for 8 hours.

2. Remove the chicken legs and allow to cool enough to remove the meat from the bone. Leave the cover off of the slow cooker and allow the onion mixture to continue to cook until the liquid has totally evaporated. (You can raise the setting to high to speed things up if you wish. Just be sure to stir the mixture occasionally to prevent the onions from burning.) Stir the chicken into the onion mixture. Add pepper.

South African–Style Chicken

SERVES 6

Cooking spray

6 boneless, skinless chicken breasts

½ cup barbecue sauce

½ cup Chicken Broth (see recipe in Chapter 2)

1 medium onion, peeled and diced

½ cup dried apricots, halved

½ cup golden raisins

1 tablespoon curry powder

1 teaspoon coriander powder

½ teaspoon ground cinnamon

2 garlic cloves, peeled and minced

3 cups cooked couscous

1. Lightly spray the inside of a 4-quart slow cooker with cooking spray. Place chicken in the slow cooker in a single layer, overlapping to fit if necessary.

2. In a medium bowl, combine the remaining ingredients except the couscous, and pour over chicken. Cover and cook on low for 8 hours. Serve over couscous.

Tamales with Chicken and Olives

SERVES 6

1 tablespoon butter

1 tablespoon flour

1 cup Chicken Broth (see recipe in Chapter 2)

1 cup olives, pitted

1 pound boneless chicken meat

1 cup tomato purée

1 cup corn

¼ cup raisins

½ teaspoon salt

2 teaspoons chili powder

8 large tamales (or 16 small)

½ cup shredded Monterey jack cheese

1. Melt the butter in a saucepan over low heat; add the flour and stir to blend and thicken. Add the Chicken Broth and mix until smooth over low heat.

2. Mince the olives and cube the chicken meat. Add the olives, chicken, tomato purée, corn, raisins, salt, and chili powder to the thickened chicken sauce.

3. Remove the husks from the tamales and arrange the tamales in the slow cooker. Top each layer of tamales with equal amounts sauce and cheese.

4. Cover and heat on a low setting for 3–4 hours.

Slow Cooker Suggestions

Recipes including fresh milk, cream, or cheese may require the dairy product to be added only at or near the end. Extended periods of cooking can cause dairy products to separate. An acidic broth, such as a tomato-based one, can have a similar effect.

Appendix A: Equipment Sources

All-Clad
www.all-clad.com/Electrics/c/electrics_category

Bella Linea
https://bellahousewares.com/products-bella

Breville
www.brevilleusa.com/collections/pressure-slow-cookers

Crock-Pot
www.crock-pot.com/slow-cookers/

Cuisinart
www.cuisinart.com/products/slow_cookers_rice_cookers

Hamilton Beach
www.hamiltonbeach.com/slow-cookers

KitchenAid
www.kitchenaid.com/countertop-appliances/slow-cookers

Maxi-Matic
www.maxi-matic.com/cooking/slow-cookers.html

Waring
www.waringpro.com

Appendix B: US/Metric Conversion Chart

VOLUME CONVERSIONS

US Volume Measure	Metric Equivalent
⅛ teaspoon	0.5 milliliter
¼ teaspoon	1 milliliter
½ teaspoon	2 milliliters
1 teaspoon	5 milliliters
½ tablespoon	7 milliliters
1 tablespoon (3 teaspoons)	15 milliliters
2 tablespoons (1 fluid ounce)	30 milliliters
¼ cup (4 tablespoons)	60 milliliters
⅓ cup	90 milliliters
½ cup (4 fluid ounces)	125 milliliters
⅔ cup	160 milliliters
¾ cup (6 fluid ounces)	180 milliliters
1 cup (16 tablespoons)	250 milliliters
1 pint (2 cups)	500 milliliters
1 quart (4 cups)	1 liter (about)

WEIGHT CONVERSIONS

US Weight Measure	Metric Equivalent
½ ounce	15 grams
1 ounce	30 grams
2 ounces	60 grams
3 ounces	85 grams
¼ pound (4 ounces)	115 grams
½ pound (8 ounces)	225 grams
¾ pound (12 ounces)	340 grams
1 pound (16 ounces)	454 grams

OVEN TEMPERATURE CONVERSIONS

Degrees Fahrenheit	Degrees Celsius
200 degrees F	95 degrees C
250 degrees F	120 degrees C
275 degrees F	135 degrees C
300 degrees F	150 degrees C
325 degrees F	160 degrees C
350 degrees F	180 degrees C
375 degrees F	190 degrees C
400 degrees F	205 degrees C
425 degrees F	220 degrees C
450 degrees F	230 degrees C

BAKING PAN SIZES

American	Metric
8 x 1½ inch round baking pan	20 x 4 cm cake tin
9 x 1½ inch round baking pan	23 x 3.5 cm cake tin
11 x 7 x 1½ inch baking pan	28 x 18 x 4 cm baking tin
13 x 9 x 2 inch baking pan	30 x 20 x 5 cm baking tin
2 quart rectangular baking dish	30 x 20 x 3 cm baking tin
15 x 10 x 2 inch baking pan	30 x 25 x 2 cm baking tin (Swiss roll tin)
9 inch pie plate	22 x 4 or 23 x 4 cm pie plate
7 or 8 inch springform pan	18 or 20 cm springform or loose bottom cake tin
9 x 5 x 3 inch loaf pan	23 x 13 x 7 cm or 2 lb narrow loaf or pate tin
1½ quart casserole	1.5 liter casserole
2 quart casserole	2 liter casserole

INDEX

American dishes, classics. *See* Classic American dishes

Appetizers, 31–42
  about: Poached Chicken suggestion, 20
  Chicken Bites, 33
  Chicken Chowder, 41
  Chicken Meatballs in a Hawaiian-Inspired Sauce, 35
  Chicken Tetrazzini, 41
  Coconut Chicken Fingers, 37
  Curried Chicken Dip, 39
  Curried Chicken Meatballs with Tomatoes, 38
  Ground Chicken Tomato Sauce, 40
  Honey-Mustard Chicken Fingers, 34
  Hot Chicken Buffalo Bites, 33
  Light and Creamy Swedish Meatballs, 36
  Spicy Buffalo Nuggets with Ranch Dressing, 42
  Stuffed Grape Leaves, 32

Apple cider chicken, spiced, 27
Artichokes, dishes with, 137, 144, 145, 152
Asian-inspired dishes, 103–12
  Almond Chicken, 111
  Almond Chicken Spinach Rolls, 112
  Asian-Spiced Chicken Breast, 112
  Chicken in Plum Sauce, 110
  Chicken with Mango-Lime Sauce, 110
  Coconut Mango Spiced Chicken, 104
  Curried Chicken in Coconut Milk, 105
  Curried Coconut Chicken with Rice, 105
  Ginger Caramelized Chicken, 108
  Orange Chicken, 109
  Teriyaki Chicken, 104
  Thai Curried Chicken, 106
  Thai-Influenced Braised Chicken Thighs, 107
  Thai Peanut Chicken, 107

Bacon, precooked and crumbled, 63
Baking, about, 13–14
Balsamic Chicken and Spinach, 148
Barbecue chicken dishes, 90, 94, 98

Basil, making pesto with, 138
Beans and other legumes. *See also* Chickpeas; Green beans
  about: white (navy) beans, 139
  Barbecue Chicken and Beans, 94
  California Chili, 68
  Chicken Chili Verde, 70
  Chicken-Tomatillo Chili, 77
  Eastern North Carolina Brunswick Stew, 72
  Easy Chicken and Rice Chili, 76
  Fiery Chicken Chili, 66
  Herbed Chicken and Vegetable Soup, 64
  Lean Green Chili, 67
  Spicy Sausage Chili, 68
  Summer Chili, 69
  Tuscan Chicken and White Beans, 139
Beef, in Chicken Stew with Meat Sauce, 78
Beer, recipes with, 23, 102
Braising/braised chicken, 14, 23, 107
Broccoli
  Chicken, Broccoli, and Rice Casserole, 87
  Creole Chicken and Vegetables, 91
  No-Crust Chicken Potpie, 81
  "Teekha" Peanut Chicken, 115
  Thai Curried Chicken, 106
  Thai Peanut Chicken, 107
Broths, chicken, 19
Broths, homemade or bases, 15
Budapest, chicken, 154
Buffalo chicken bites, hot, 33
Buffalo Chicken Sandwich Filling, 95
Buffalo Chicken Wings, 45
Buffalo nuggets, spicy, 42
Buying slow cooker, 10

Cabbage, in Chicken Fricassee, 148
Cabbage Rollatini, 135
Cacciatore, chicken, 85
Cajun Chicken and Shrimp Creole, 99
California Chili, 68
Capers, about, 146
Caramel syrup, making, 108

Caribbean Chicken Curry, 156
Caring for slow cookers, 12–13
Carrot quiche, ground chicken and, 29
Cauliflower, dishes with, 81, 91, 135
Cheese
    about: Cotija, 159
    parmesan. See Italian-inspired dishes
    Sage Ricotta Chicken Breasts, 150
    Sun-Dried Tomato and Feta–Stuffed
        Chicken, 147
Chickpeas, dishes with, 59, 129, 161
Chili Coconut Chicken (Mangalorian Murgh
    Gassi), 120
Chilis and stews, 65–78
    about: Brunswick Stew origins, 72; liquid
        smoke and, 66; making rice while chili
        cooks, 70
    California Chili, 68
    Chicken and Mushroom Stew, 74
    Chicken and Sweet Potato Stew, 71
    Chicken Chili Verde, 70
    Chicken Chowder, 41
    Chicken Corn Chowder, 71
    Chicken Stew with Meat Sauce, 78
    Chicken-Tomatillo Chili, 77
    Creamy Chicken Stew, 73
    Eastern North Carolina Brunswick Stew,
        72
    Easy Chicken and Rice Chili, 76
    Ethiopian Chicken Stew, 162
    Fiery Chicken Chili, 66
    Lean Green Chili, 67
    Rosemary-Thyme Stew, 75
    Spicy Sausage Chili, 68
    Summer Chili, 69
    Tuscan Chicken and Sausage Stew, 74
Cinnamon Chicken Pasta, 81
Citrus
    Chicken in Lemon Sauce, 86
    Chicken with Mango-Lime Sauce, 110
    Greek Lemon-Chicken Soup, 57
    Lemony Roast Chicken, 151
    Orange Chicken, 109
Classic American dishes, 91–102
    Barbecue Chicken and Beans, 94
    Buffalo Chicken Sandwich Filling, 95
    Cajun Chicken and Shrimp Creole, 99
    Chicken Taco Filling, 100
    Chicken Tenders, 97

Chili Beer Chicken, 102
Creole Chicken and Vegetables, 92
Enchilada Filling, Paleo Style, 101
Ground Chicken Joes, 96
Hawaiian Chicken, 93
Molasses Barbecue Chicken, 98
Salsa Chicken, 102
Saucy Brown Sugar Chicken, 97
Sweet and Spicy Pulled Chicken, 95
Cleaning slow cookers, 12–13
Coconut
    Chili Coconut Chicken (Mangalorian
        Murgh Gassi), 120
    Coconut Chicken Fingers, 37
    Coconut Mango Spiced Chicken, 104
    Curried Chicken in Coconut Milk, 105
    Curried Coconut Chicken with Rice, 105
    Thai Curried Chicken, 106
Comforting Chicken and Rice Soup, 53
Comforting favorites, 79–90
    Barbecue Chicken, 90
    Biscuit-Topped Chicken Pie, 82
    Chicken, Broccoli, and Rice Casserole, 87
    Chicken and Dumplings, 80
    Chicken and Gravy, 83
    Chicken Cacciatore, 85
    Chicken in Lemon Sauce, 86
    Chicken Paprikash, 88
    Chicken Stroganoff, 84
    Cinnamon Chicken Pasta, 81
    Creamy Chicken in a Mushroom and
        White Wine Sauce, 89
    Easy Chicken and Dressing, 83
    Honey-Mustard Chicken, 90
    No-Crust Chicken Potpie, 81
    Scalloped Chicken, 84
Congee, chicken, 59
Cooking terms, 13–14
Coriander Chicken (Dhaniye Wala Murgh),
    121
Corn
    Chicken Corn Chowder, 71
    Chicken Pesto Polenta, 138
    Creamy Chicken Stew, 73
    Eastern North Carolina Brunswick Stew,
        72
    Herbed Chicken and Vegetable Soup, 64
    Summer Chili, 69
    Tamales with Chicken and Olives, 166

Tortilla Soup, 54
Creamy Chicken in a Mushroom and White Wine Sauce, 89
Creamy Chicken Stew, 73
Creamy sauce, chicken in (Murgh Korma), 119
Creole Chicken and Vegetables, 92
Cucumber soup, Vietnamese, 60
Curries. See also Asian-inspired dishes; Indian-inspired dishes
  about: serving garnishes with, 61; turmeric benefits and, 39
  Caribbean Chicken Curry, 156
  Chicken Mulligatawny Soup, 61
  Curried Chicken Dip, 39
  Curried Chicken Meatballs with Tomatoes, 38
  Green Curry Wings, 44

Dredging, about, 140
Dressing, easy chicken and, 83
Drumsticks. See Wings and drumsticks
Dumplings, chicken and, 80

Easy, essential recipes, 17–29
  Chicken and Gherkin Sandwich, 29
  Chicken Braised in Beer, 23
  Chicken Broth, 19
  Chicken in Onion-Mushroom Gravy, 26
  Chicken Stock, 18
  Foolproof Chicken, 22
  Ground Chicken and Carrot Quiche, 29
  Mushroom Chicken Breast, 25
  Poached Chicken, 20
  "Precooked" Chicken, 20
  Roast Chicken, 22
  Rotisserie-Style Chicken, 21
  Spiced Apple Cider Chicken, 27
  Spicy Plum Chicken, 24
  Spicy Roasted Chicken Breast, 27
  Steamed Chicken Sandwich, 23
  Wild Rice–Stuffed Chicken Breast Cutlets, 28
Eggs, Ground Chicken and Carrot Quiche, 29
Enchilada Filling, Paleo Style, 101
Ethiopian Chicken Stew, 162

Fenugreek-Flavored Chicken (Murgh Methiwala), 122
Fiery Chicken Chili, 66
Figs, chicken with, 160
Filipino Chicken Adobo, 164
Fingers, Coconut, 37
Fingers, honey-mustard, 34
Five-Ingredient Greek Chicken, 152
Flavors, enhancing/correcting, 15
Frozen meat, using, 16

Garlic Chicken (Lehsun Wala), 124
Ginger Caramelized Chicken, 108
Ginger-Flavored Chicken Curry (Murgh Adraki), 123
Gluten-free, checking about processed foods, 92
Gluten-Free "Shake It and Bake It" Drumsticks, 48
Gluten-free stuffing, drumsticks with, 50
Goan Chicken Curry, 115
Grape leaves, stuffed, 32
Gravy, chicken and, 83
Gravy, Rotisserie-Style Chicken, 21
Greek Lemon-Chicken Soup, 57
Greek-Style Orzo and Spinach Soup, 55
Green beans
  Chicken in Lemon Sauce, 86
  Eastern North Carolina Brunswick Stew, 72
  Herbed Chicken and Vegetable Soup, 64
  Slow Cooker Chicken with Green Beans, 137
  Tuscan Chicken and Sausage Stew, 74
Green Chutney Wings, 47
Green Curry Wings, 44
Ground Chicken and Carrot Quiche, 29
Ground Chicken Joes, 96
Ground Chicken Tomato Sauce, 40

Hawaiian Chicken, 93
Herbed Chicken and Vegetable Soup, 64
Herbs to use, 15–16
Honey-Glazed Chicken Drumsticks, 49
Honey-Mustard Chicken, 90
Honey-Mustard Chicken Fingers, 34
Honey Mustard Dipping Sauce, 37
Honey wings, sticky, 44
Hot Chicken Buffalo Bites, 33

Indian-inspired dishes, 113–29
    about: oils/ghee used in cooking, 123
    Almond-Flavored Chicken (Badami
        Murgh), 117
    Chicken Curry with Red Potatoes, 118
    Chicken in a Creamy Sauce (Murgh
        Korma), 119
    Chicken Makhani, 114
    Chicken Mulligatawny Soup, 61
    Chicken Tikka Masala, 116
    Chicken with Pickling Spices (Murgh
        Achari), 125
    Chili Coconut Chicken (Mangalorian
        Murgh Gassi), 120
    Coriander Chicken (Dhaniye Wala Murgh),
        121
    Fenugreek-Flavored Chicken (Murgh
        Methiwala), 122
    Garlic Chicken (Lehsun Wala), 124
    Ginger-Flavored Chicken Curry (Murgh
        Adraki), 123
    Goan Chicken Curry, 115
    Indian Chicken with Chickpea Sauce, 129
    Murghi ka Shorba (Chicken Soup), 56
    Murgh Musallam, 126
    Slow Cooker Tandoori Chicken, 127
    Spiced Chicken in Green Curry (Murgh
        Hariyali), 128
    Tandoori Chicken Wings, 46
    "Teekha" Peanut Chicken, 115
International favorites, 155–66. See also
    Asian-inspired dishes; Indian-inspired
    dishes; Italian-inspired dishes; Mediterra-
    nean-inspired dishes
    Caribbean Chicken Curry, 156
    Chicken in Onion Sauce, 164
    Chicken with Figs, 160
    Ethiopian Chicken Stew, 162
    Filipino Chicken Adobo, 164
    Jerk Chicken, 162
    Moroccan Chicken, 161
    Peruvian Chicken with Aji Verde, 159
    Peruvian Roast Chicken with Red Pota-
        toes, 158
    South African–Style Chicken, 165
    Spanish Chicken and Rice, 157
    Tamales with Chicken and Olives, 166
    Tarragon Chicken, 163
Italian-inspired dishes, 131–42

Cabbage Rollatini, 135
Chicken Alfredo Pasta, 137
Chicken Meatball Sun-Dried Tomato
    Sauce, 141
Chicken Parmesan, 133
Chicken Pesto Polenta, 138
Chicken Piccata, 140
Chicken Ragu, 133
Chicken Saltimbocca, 134
Italian Chicken, 136
Italian Chicken Meatloaf, 142
Pesto Chicken, 132
Shortcut Chicken Parmesan, 132
Slow Cooker Chicken with Green Beans,
    137
Tomato and Chicken Sausage Sauce, 134
Tuscan Chicken, 136
Tuscan Chicken and White Beans, 139

Jerk Chicken, 162
Joes, ground chicken, 96

Maintaining/caring for slow cookers, 12–13
Mango, dishes with, 104, 110
Measuring cup, microwave-safe, 15
Meatballs, 35, 36, 38, 141
Meatloaf, Italian chicken, 142
Mediterranean-inspired dishes, 143–54
    Balsamic Chicken and Spinach, 148
    Chicken and Artichokes, 145
    Chicken Budapest, 154
    Chicken Cutlets with Red Onion Sauce,
        152
    Chicken Fricassee, 148
    Five-Ingredient Greek Chicken, 152
    Lemony Roast Chicken, 151
    Mediterranean Chicken Casserole, 145
    Roast Chicken with Lemon and Arti-
        chokes, 144
    Rosemary Chicken with Potatoes, 149
    Sage Ricotta Chicken Breasts, 150
    Slow-Roasted Chicken with Potatoes,
        Parsnips, and Onions, 153
    Spicy Olive Chicken, 146
    Sun-Dried Tomato and Feta–Stuffed
        Chicken, 147
Mint, dishes using, 32, 128
Molasses Barbecue Chicken, 98
Moroccan Chicken, 161

Mulligatawny soup, 61
Murgh/Murghi. *See* Indian-inspired dishes
Mushrooms
    Chicken and Mushroom Stew, 74
    Chicken in Onion-Mushroom Gravy, 26
    Creamy Chicken in a Mushroom and
       White Wine Sauce, 89
    Herbed Chicken and Vegetable Soup, 64
    Mushroom Chicken Breast, 25

Nuggets, spicy buffalo, 42
Nuts
    about: toasting almonds, 111
    Almond Chicken, 111
    Almond Chicken Spinach Rolls, 112
    Almond-Flavored Chicken (Badami
       Murgh), 117
    "Teekha" Peanut Chicken, 115
    Thai Peanut Chicken, 107

Oils, 49, 123, 125
Olive chicken, spicy, 146
Olives, tamales with chicken and, 166
Onions
    Chicken Cutlets with Red Onion Sauce,
       152
    Chicken in Onion-Mushroom Gravy, 26
    Chicken in Onion Sauce, 164
    Slow-Roasted Chicken with Potatoes,
       Parsnips, and Onions, 153

Paprikash, chicken, 88
Parmesan, chicken with. *See* Italian-inspired
    dishes
Parsnips, dishes with, 18, 80, 82, 153
Pasta
    about: Ground Chicken Joes over, 96
    Chicken Alfredo Pasta, 137
    Chicken Noodle Soup, 52
    Chicken Paprikash, 88
    Chicken Soup with Lukshen (Noodles), 62
    Chicken Stroganoff, 84
    Chicken with Mango-Lime Sauce, 110
    Cinnamon Chicken Pasta, 81
    Creamy Chicken in a Mushroom and
       White Wine Sauce, 89
    Greek-Style Orzo and Spinach Soup, 55
    "Precooked" Chicken with, 20
    Tuscan Chicken and White Beans with, 139

Peanuts. *See* Nuts
Peruvian dishes, 158, 159
Pesto, chicken with, 132, 138
Picatta, chicken, 140
Pickling spices, chicken with (Murgh Achari),
    125
Pies, savory, 81, 82
Pineapple, dishes with, 35, 47, 93
Plum chicken, spicy, 24
Plum sauce, chicken in, 110
Poached Chicken, 20
Polenta, chicken pesto, 138
Potatoes
    about: Ground Chicken Joes over, 96
    Chicken Curry with Red Potatoes, 118
    Chicken in Onion-Mushroom Gravy, 26
    Herbed Chicken and Vegetable Soup, 64
    Honey-Mustard Chicken, 90
    Peruvian Roast Chicken with Red Pota-
       toes, 158
    Pesto Chicken, 132
    Roast Chicken, 22
    Rosemary Chicken with Potatoes, 149
    Rosemary-Thyme Stew, 75
    Scalloped Chicken, 84
    Slow-Roasted Chicken with Potatoes,
       Parsnips, and Onions, 153
Potpie, no-crust chicken, 81
"Precooked" Chicken, 20
Pulled chicken, sweet and spicy, 95

Ragu, chicken, 133
Recipes. *See also specific recipes*
    broth bases, homemade broths and, 15
    cooking terms to know, 13–14
    cutting chicken and veggies for, 11
    enhancing/correcting flavors, 15
    frozen vs. fresh meat, 16
    herbs to use, 15–16
    making each dish your own, 14–16
    microwave-safe measuring cup for, 15
    spice/aromatic vegetable characteristics
       and, 12
    thawing food and, 12
    time required for cooking, 12
    water and, 11
Rice and wild rice
    about: cooking whole grain brown rice,
       105; Ground Chicken Joes over, 96;

Rice and wild rice—*continued*
  making rice while chili cooks, 70
  Aromatic Chicken Rice Soup, 58
  Barbecue Chicken and Beans, 94
  Chicken, Broccoli, and Rice Casserole, 87
  Chicken and Wild Rice Soup, 63
  Chicken Congee, 59
  Comforting Chicken and Rice Soup, 53
  Creole Chicken and Vegetables, 92
  Curried Coconut Chicken with Rice, 105
  Easy Chicken and Rice Chili, 76
  Greek Lemon-Chicken Soup, 57
  Mediterranean Chicken Casserole, 145
  Spanish Chicken and Rice, 157
  Tuscan Chicken and White Beans with, 139
  Wild Rice–Stuffed Chicken Breast Cutlets, 28
Roast Chicken, 22
Roasted chicken breast, spicy, 27
Rosemary Chicken with Potatoes, 149
Rosemary-Thyme Stew, 75
Rotisserie-Style Chicken, 21

Sage Ricotta Chicken Breasts, 150
Salads
  about: "Precooked" Chicken for, 20
Salsa Chicken, 102
Saltimbocca, chicken, 134
Sandwiches
  Buffalo Chicken Sandwich Filling, 95
  Chicken and Gherkin Sandwich, 29
  Ground Chicken Joes, 96
  Steamed Chicken Sandwich, 23
Sauces
  about: chili sauce and chili-garlic sauce, 44; Greek-style yogurt dipping sauce, 32; liquid smoke and, 66; making barbecue sauce, 94; making caramel syrup, 108; Peruvian dipping sauce, 158; Rotisserie-Style Chicken gravy, 21
  Chicken Meatball Sun-Dried Tomato Sauce, 141
  Curried Chicken Dip, 39
  Ground Chicken Tomato Sauce, 40
  Hawaiian-Inspired Sauce, 35
  Honey Mustard Dipping Sauce, 37
  Mushroom and White Wine Sauce, 89
  Onion-Mushroom Gravy, 26
  Ranch Dressing, 42
  Tomato and Chicken Sausage Sauce, 134
Saucy Brown Sugar Chicken, 97
Sautéing, 14, 15
Scalloped Chicken, 84
Shortcut Chicken Parmesan, 132
Shrimp, in Cajun Chicken and Shrimp Creole, 99
Slow cookers
  about: getting started using, 9
  buying, 10, 167
  caring for, 12–13
  cooking poultry with, 142
  cooking terms to know, 13–14
  cutting up ingredients for, 11
  features and options, 10
  heating up/maintaining heat, 11
  lifting cover, 11
  liners for, 13
  multiple, for several main dishes/making ahead, 97
  placing ingredients in, 11
  spice/aromatic vegetable characteristics and, 12
  temperature ranges, 10–11
  time required for cooking, 12
  tips to remember, 11–12
  using, 10–12
Soups, 51–64. *See also* Chilis and stews
  about: bouquet garni for, 62
  Aromatic Chicken Rice Soup, 58
  Chicken and Wild Rice Soup, 63
  Chicken Congee, 59
  Chicken Mulligatawny Soup, 61
  Chicken Noodle Soup, 52
  Chicken Soup with Lukshen (Noodles), 62
  Chicken Vegetable Soup, 55
  Comforting Chicken and Rice Soup, 53
  Greek Lemon-Chicken Soup, 57
  Greek-Style Orzo and Spinach Soup, 55
  Herbed Chicken and Vegetable Soup, 64
  Murghi ka Shorba (Chicken Soup), 56
  Simple Ground Chicken and Vegetable Soup, 58
  Tlalpeno Soup, 59
  Tortilla Soup, 54
  Vietnamese Cucumber Soup, 60
South African–Style Chicken, 165
Spanish Chicken and Rice, 157

Spiced Apple Cider Chicken, 27
Spicy Buffalo Nuggets with Ranch Dressing, 42
Spicy Olive Chicken, 146
Spicy Plum Chicken, 24
Spicy Roasted Chicken Breast, 27
Spicy Sausage Chili, 68
Spinach, dishes with, 55, 112, 148
Steamed Chicken Sandwich, 23
Stewing, about, 14
Stews. See Chilis and stews
Sticky Honey Wings, 44
Stock, chicken, 18
Stroganoff, chicken, 84
Stuffed Grape Leaves, 32
Summer Chili, 69
Swedish meatballs, light and creamy, 36
Sweet and Spicy Pulled Chicken, 95
Sweet potatoes
    Chicken and Sweet Potato Stew, 71
    Chicken with Figs, 71
    Spiced Apple Cider Chicken, 27

Taco filling, 100
Tamales with Chicken and Olives, 166
Tandoori Chicken Wings, 46
Tandoori dishes. See Indian-inspired dishes
Tarragon Chicken, 163
"Teekha" Peanut Chicken, 115
Tenders, chicken, 97
Teriyaki Chicken, 104
Teriyaki drumsticks, pineapple, 47
Tetrazzini, chicken, 41
Thai dishes. See Asian-inspired dishes
Tlalpeno Soup, 59
Tomatillos, in Chicken-Tomatillo Chili, 77
Tomatoes
    about: sun-dried, 141
    Curried Chicken Meatballs with Tomatoes, 38
    sauces with. See Sauces
    soups and stews with. See Chilis and stews; Soups
    Sun-Dried Tomato and Feta–Stuffed Chicken, 147
Tortilla Soup, 54
Tuscan Chicken, 136
Tuscan Chicken and Sausage Stew, 74
Tuscan Chicken and White Beans, 139

Vegetables. See also specific vegetables
    about: cutting for slow cooker, 11; placement in slow cooker, 11; sautéing, 14, 15
    Biscuit-Topped Chicken Pie, 82
    Chicken Broth, 19
    Chicken Stock, 18
    Creole Chicken and Vegetables, 92
    No-Crust Chicken Potpie, 81
    soups and stews with. See Chilis and stews; Soups
Vietnamese Cucumber Soup, 60

Wild rice. See Rice and wild rice
Wings and drumsticks, 43–50
    Buffalo Chicken Wings, 45
    Chicken Drumsticks with Gluten-Free Stuffing, 50
    Gluten-Free "Shake It and Bake It" Drumsticks, 48
    Green Chutney Wings, 47
    Green Curry Wings, 44
    Honey-Glazed Chicken Drumsticks, 49
    Pineapple Teriyaki Drumsticks, 47
    Sassy and Sweet Chicken Wings, 45
    Sticky Honey Wings, 44
    Tandoori Chicken Wings, 46

Yogurt, about Greek, 114